America's Economic Supremacy

by BROOKS ADAMS

With a New Evaluation by Marquis W. Childs

Nearly fifty years ago Brooks Adams, one of this country's greatest interpreters of the ebb and flow of world power, called the turn of today's international crisis. He forecast England's fall as a dominating state, the shift in the centers of power to the east and to the west, the rise of Russia and America as the two great opposing nations and their rivalry for world supremacy. At the height of an era of optimism and complacency he called for a realistic acceptance of a dreadful national responsibility.

Written with vigor and clarity, Brooks Adams' is a vastly thought provoking book on trends in the modern world— *on the real and shocking facts which must be faced by every American today.* theories to the world of today and points out the importance of Adams' remarkable forecasts.

AMERICA'S
ECONOMIC SUPREMACY

AMERICA'S
Economic Supremacy

BY

Brooks Adams

With a New Evaluation by

MARQUIS W. CHILDS

HARPER & BROTHERS PUBLISHERS
New York and London

10-7

AMERICA'S ECONOMIC SUPREMACY

FIRST EDITION

H-W

Contents

America's Economic Supremacy is reprinted by the kind permission of Mr. Henry Adams of Boston.

EVALUATION

Evaluation

By Marquis W. Childs

THIS book was first published in 1900. It had only a negligible sale, and the reviewers who noticed it seemed to have no idea what Brooks Adams was trying to say. He was going against the tide of optimism that in America carried everything with it at the end of the nineteenth century. This in itself confirmed the suspicion that the author was an eccentric theorist determined to maintain a kind of quaint professional pessimism.

If Adams had written last year, for publication this year, he would have had to alter scarcely anything to relate his views to the world of today. That is a measure of the prescience of *America's Economic Supremacy*. The present text is complete with the exception of one chapter that seemed to be a piece of literary criticism irrelevant to the main objective of the book and the elimination of over-long military detail in the chapter on the Boer War.

Brooks Adams in 1900 foresaw a world in which

there would be only two powers, Russia and the United States. He foresaw with extraordinary clarity the rise of our economic supremacy. He understood so well how far-reaching would be the consequences of that supremacy. If we failed to comprehend its meaning in terms of responsibility, the results would be as momentous as though we used or misused that accretion of power.

The author of *America's Economic Supremacy* was a prophet not without honor, save in his own land. His work was accorded more serious critical attention in Europe than in this country. The reader today will marvel at Adams' vision at the same time that he recognizes the limits on his thought. His prophecies have been realized in such magnitude that his suggested solutions for America's dilemma seem almost as inadequate as those that greeted us in the headlines of yesterday's newspaper.

In 1895 Adams published his *Law of Civilization and Decay*. That developed the theme at the heart of all his thinking. After long study of economic trends, he became convinced that the center of trade had consistently followed a westward movement from the ancient crossroads in the East to Constantinople, Venice, Amsterdam, and finally London. This movement occurred in accord with a law relating to the density of populations and the development of new and centralizing techniques of trade and industry.

The essays that make up the present book are, in one sense, an application of that law. Adams traces the beginnings of England's decline and the rise of America's supremacy. He views this change with a bleak detachment that owes something to his New England origins. It owes more, however, to the scientific determinism that colored so much of the thinking of his time.

On the rise of Russian power he was less definite. In general, however, he believed that this would result from two factors: one, the consolidation of Russia's vast land mass and, indeed, the very weight of that mass; and, two, the integration of Russia and Germany. Adams does not make it clear how this last might come about. But he seems to regard it almost as a certainty that the fusion of Slav mass and power with Prussian drive and organizing capacity would take place. We in our time can see how nearly this remarkable prophecy was correct.

Brooks Adams' career parallels that of his brother, Henry, in many ways. They were both acutely conscious of their family background and the chain that linked them with great events in America's past. They both wrote history. They both traveled from place to place with a restless unease. They both showed toward most people a shyness and reserve which was compounded with arrogance and often, in Brooks, with a combativeness and a desire for argument for the sake of argument that sorely tried Henry.

Out of their relationship, carried on mainly by correspondence, grew the idea that each was to develop in his own way. That idea, so revolutionary for the day, was that by its nature and substance American democracy was almost foreordained to degradation and decay. This fate was closely related to the ever more disastrous working of the economic cycle, particularly as it was affected by the fantastically swift development of new invention and technology. These strange brothers, joined by their belief in a threatening doom, were, as Henry once put it, like physicians taking the pulse of a patient on the edge of dissolution.

Brooks Adams, the youngest son of Charles Francis Adams, was born on June 24, 1848. He had the conventional education of an upper-class Bostonian, including undergraduate work and one year of law at Harvard, an institution for which both Brooks and Henry expressed in later years nothing but scorn. For a time Brooks was in London during the troubled years of the Civil War when his father was trying, as minister to England, to keep Great Britain from recognizing the Confederacy.

He was, however, much too young to get the view

of this experience that was to exert such an influence on Henry. In that gifted family Brooks occupied an anomalous position. Henry was recognized as the philosopher and the aesthete. Charles Francis, Jr., the only son to go into business, became president of the Union Pacific Railroad. Brooks was considered something of an eccentric. Neither by his immediate family nor by his friends was he taken very seriously.

Outwardly, Brooks's life was conventional enough. In 1889 he married Evelyn Davis, daughter of Admiral Charles Henry Davis and sister of Mrs. Henry Cabot Lodge. Thanks to a large inheritance from their maternal grandfather, Peter Chardon Brooks, as well as to fortunate investments and good marriages, all the Adams' had ample independent incomes. Brooks Adams and his wife traveled in Europe, the Middle East, and India. He was constantly in pursuit of facts and figures with which to document his theory of history.

He published enough to establish his reputation as an iconoclast. Such a reputation was not difficult to achieve in that time and that environment. His first book, *The Emancipation of Massachusetts*, went a long way toward shattering the concept of the settlement of the Massachusetts Bay Colony as a movement motivated solely by idealism and directed by Puritan saints.

In 1893 an event occurred which shook the Adams family to its foundations. In the panic of that year the Adams' very nearly lost their fortunes. Henry was fifty-five years old. The tragedy of his wife's death had, as he believed, severed his life. In his letters he wrote of himself as a kind of shadow sentenced to live out the remaining years with all purpose and reason gone. Brooks and Henry spent most of that summer together in the old Adams house at Quincy. Brooks has described how they talked through those summer nights of the meaning of the financial crisis that racked the nation. While they considered what this might do to them personally, they put it aside with a Puritan disdain. Their personal fortunes—they were both childless—seemed to matter so little against the vast sweep of world history, the concatenation of events moving toward a climax which they began dimly to discern.

But at the same time it was characteristic of Brooks, and to a lesser degree of Henry, to reduce history to the figuration of the Adams family. The setting was perfect. The house at Quincy was a kind of stage on which two American presidents had acted the drama of their early years. It spoke of the minds and the wills that had forged the Revolution. History, and the austerity and the vigor of the New England spirit of an earlier day, was in every beam of it. Here were the Adams archives, masses of letters, diaries, notebooks, semipublic papers; a mass which appalled Henry and tended to awe Brooks.

Seeking the causes of the panic and its meaning for the future, Brooks went back to his grandfather, John Quincy Adams, the sixth president of the United States. He went back to a memorandum in which John Quincy Adams had outlined a program for the development of the resources of the nation. It was a document characteristic of the sixth president. He had labored over it with the greatest care. It offered a reasonable, orderly course for the gradual exploitation of the incalculable wealth of the still largely undeveloped continent. As John Quincy Adams conceived it, the Federal Government would have to exercise the most careful control over this wealth in order to prevent reckless waste and the enrichment of the few at the expense of the many through speculation and other abuses.

It was characteristic of John Quincy Adams that he could advance such a program as though it undoubtedly had a chance of adoption. Given the temper of the times, the booming outward thrust of an expanding people into a wilderness of natural wealth that must be inexhaustible, Federal restraints were the last thing that anyone desired. As with so many of John Quincy Adams' state papers, the memorandum on natural resources was merely an exercise in stern intellectuality.

It was characteristic of Brooks Adams that he should take the rejection of his grandfather's program as a turning point in America's history. He saw it as the last attempt to prevent the ruthless exploitation of the continent by spoil and pillage. The symbol of that exploitation, for an Adams, was Andrew Jackson, who had defeated John Quincy Adams when he ran for re-election. Prejudices ran strong in the Adams family, and Brooks saw in Jackson the embodiment of the spoils system, surrender to the base instincts of greed and cupidity.

As they talked through the summer evenings, Brooks and Henry agreed that the exaltation of the profit motive above everything else had degraded all values and therefore had degraded American life. Or at any rate, Brooks says that they agreed. Henry was far more cautious about expressing such heretical opinions. He was even more cautious than his brother, Charles Francis, who was part of the business world. These Adams' had an ingrained sense of public duty and common obligation that made them reject the slack and spurious mores of the men who were amassing quick fortunes. In his *Main Currents of American*

Thought Vernon Parrington quotes the following from Charles Francis' autobiography:

Indeed, as I approach the end, I am more than a little puzzled to account for the instances I have seen of business success—money getting. It comes from a rather low instinct. Certainly, as far as my observation goes, it is rarely met with in combination with the finer or more interesting traits of character. I have known, and known tolerably well, a good many "successful" men—"big" financially—men famous during the last half-century; and a less interesting crowd I do not care to encounter. Not one that I have ever known would I care to meet again, either in this world or the next; nor is one of them associated in my mind with the idea of humor, thought, or refinement. A set of mere money-getters and traders, they were essentially unattractive and uninteresting. . . . In the course of my railroad experiences I made no friends, apart from those in the Boston direction; nor among those I met was there any man whose acquaintance I valued. They were a coarse, realistic, bargaining crowd.

The Adams' investments were not lost. The two brothers were free to go their separate ways again; to ponder the fate of the world as it passed before their eyes. Ed Howe, of Kansas, once said that Henry Adams was the only man in America who could sit on a fence and watch himself go by. The two brothers were almost the only Americans of their day who had the detachment, the curiosity, the searching intellect, and the leisure to try to appraise the drift of events.

It was almost as though they had unearthed a secret that they scarcely dared to impart to their fellow men. The newest volume of Henry's letters, collected and edited with devoted care by Harold Dean Cater (*Henry Adams and his Friends*, Houghton Mifflin Company), shows this strange relationship more clearly than ever before.

Transfusions of gold from the Transvaal had begun to relieve Britain's position in the late 1890's. Henry and Brooks regarded this as merely a temporary expedient that might postpone the final reckoning but certainly could not avert it. Henry was in London. He wrote to Brooks telling what he had done to further interest in the *Law of Civilization and Decay*, which had just been published there, and which later received serious critical attention both in England and America.

But in America its reception was complicated by the fact that Brooks had championed the cause of free silver as opposed to the conservative moneyed interests that regarded this as the ultimate heresy. The issue of the gold standard versus the free coinage of silver was at this time being fiercely contested. Repeatedly in his letters, Henry warned Brooks against calling down the wrath of the "gold bugs" by whom he meant the group in Wall Street that dominated America's money market. The gold bugs will get you if you don't watch out, was an ever recurring theme in Henry's letters to his brother. On January 3, 1896, Henry wrote to Brooks from Washington:

The trend of this last week is still, I think, towards general disintegration abroad and the formation of a new American centre, offset by the Russian centre forming across Asia. We have practically united all America and divided Europe. . . .

This was a fateful moment in America's history, a year after the insurrection in Cuba had begun. It was the beginning of a chain of events that would project American interests into the far Pacific and involve this country irrevocably in world affairs. But the Cuban insurrection, as Brooks Adams shows clearly in *America's Economic Supremacy*, had cast its shadow long in advance. The roots of that upheaval could be traced back to the profound shift in the sugar trade, which in turn, had its origin in England's rising mercantilism and the competitive drive for low wages and low living costs. It was such interrelations that Brooks with his analytical mind was forever tracing.

In August of 1897 Henry wrote from St. Germain-en-Laye in France. He was delving deep into medieval art and history and he told Brooks that it pained him to think of the sad plight of humanity. Both brothers were closely following the struggles of the Bank of England. That Gibraltar of the nineteenth century was showing distinct signs of uneasiness. The Bank was buying gold. A rise in the Bank's interest rate of a year before had produced no gold.

Brooks and his wife were planning to go abroad in the fall. They might or might not meet Henry. These two diagnosticians of an ailing society were constantly crossing and recrossing the Atlantic. Henry was determined to escape into the cool, rose-colored gloom of Chartres and into an age that seemed to him pure and simple, and divinely beautiful in its simplicity. Brooks was bent on pursuing to their calamitous end the events that he saw happening around him. The Brooks Adams' were in Paris by Christmas of 1897. Brooks was engaged in bringing out the French edition of his *Law of Civilization and Decay*.

The following June, Henry was in London and Brooks was in Boston. The correspondence between them dealt with the mounting fever registered on the patient's economic chart. One of the most extraordinary passages occurs in a letter from Henry in the Cater collection dated June 11, 1898:

. . . The secret of all lies in the returns of the Board of Trade, which show that this year at last settles the fact that British industry is quite ruined and that its decline has at last become a debacle. France is, if possible, worse off. Germany has become a mere province of Russia. The world has entered on a new phase of most far-reaching revolution, and our only danger is lest the ruins of the old empires should tumble too quickly on America.

Brooks had a respect for his brother's intellectual powers that amounted almost to awe. The ideas that Henry expressed in his letters undoubtedly colored Brooks's thinking at this time. They were both masters of the brilliant pervasive generalization which could strip away current illusion. Henry frequently encouraged Brooks to push his studies further. In a letter written from a country retreat in England in the summer of 1898, with a flash of insight, he predicted the new polarization between Russia and the United States with England in between. What seems even more extraordinary from the perspective of a half-century later is his realization that the "central bearings" of the British Empire would of necessity come to rest in Africa. This is a fact that even informed individuals today seem scarcely to have understood.

One of the essays comprising this book appeared in the *Fortnightly Review* in the summer of 1899. Brooks sent the magazine to Henry who reproached him for pouring out with his "accustomed prodigality of mind" enough material in a short article for several volumes. Brooks was always provocative rather than definitive and nowhere more so than in *America's Economic Supremacy*. Yet it has the kind of documentation its author was forever searching out: tables, statistics, the reflection of economic trends.

In the fall of 1899 Brooks went to Dresden for a few months. Henry was in Paris. The letters that passed between the brothers were chiefly concerned with the Boer War and its meaning for England and the world. Obviously it intensified Britain's troubles, particularly in the money market. Henry predicted that it would give a new impetus to the transference of the money center westward to New York, a development which he viewed with sardonic humor. In his analysis of Britain's miserable showing against the Boers, Brooks, in the book he was to publish the following year, took an extremely pessimistic view of British military capacity and even of British stamina and courage. Events of fifteen years later were to show that he was altogether too critical. Yet from his analysis we get an idea of how the disasters of the conflict in Africa influenced the current of European history. Their meaning was not lost on Kaiser Wilhelm and the overweening military men around him who were planning far-flung conquests. Henry wrote that in the long run, by which he meant three generations, Russia and Germany working together would become "unassailable to us," the biggest mass in the most central position, and able to overwhelm America at any point of contact.

In the early spring of 1900 Brooks and his wife were about to return to America, and Henry was on the point of departing from Washington, which he found stale and boring. The brothers were in agreement that American politics were at least a hundred years behind the swiftly changing American economy and, as Henry grimly remarked, likely to remain so. In the late fall, Macmillan sent to Henry in Paris a copy of *America's Economic Supremacy*.

Brooks had hinted that his brother seemed little interested in his later work. Henry replied that if this was so, it was because he had remained primarily interested in their theory while Brooks was concerned over its application. This bit of self-analysis suggests a fundamental difference between the two. Henry's interest was exhausted when he had developed the theory to his own satisfaction and had seen what he believed to be the beginning of its confirmation in the headlines of the day. The more practical Brooks wanted to see it through to the end. From Paris, in November of the same year, Henry wrote Brooks:

It's a queer sensation, this secret belief that one stands on the brink of the world's greatest catastrophe. For it means the fall of Western Europe, as it fell in the fourth century. It recurs to me every November and culminates every December. I have to get over it as I can, and hide, for fear of being sent to an asylum. Curiously enough, I think the people, way down, have here a sense of it something like mine; but society is absolutely sane,—like Rome in the year 300. . . .

The two brothers, as the letters passed back and forth, were in disagreement. Henry's profound gloom and doubt had led him into isolationism. He had become convinced that America was utterly incapable of taking a leading part in world affairs. Therefore, he counselled letting England go down, abandoning China and the Philippines, and allowing Russia-Germany to try to run the world. Brooks, on the other hand, believed that the United States should lead the way in developing an Asiatic confederation, or imperium, perhaps, organized to exploit the markets and the natural resources of China. The latter he greatly exaggerated, as was a kind of current fashion.

What Brooks seemed to assume was that in taking on a responsibility commensurate with our economic power, we should follow the pattern of Great Britain. He did not foresee that colonial peoples everywhere would move so quickly toward independence, rejecting their colonial status both politically and economically. Nor could he foresee the enormous growth in productivity of American industry, a growth so extraordinary that it is no longer possible to talk merely in terms of exporting our surplus to undeveloped markets readily available. This last was in the tradition of the nineteenth century, a tradition that in its latter phase was dressed up with a Kiplingesque romanticism. Brooks was also influenced by the current fallacy that Asiatic peoples—and he included the Russians among them—were incapable of the kind of social organization essential in the age of the machine.

We shall have to use new forms and new techniques to help backward peoples move somewhat nearer our level if we are to find markets for our advanced technology. A radio is of no use to a Bedouin in a tent. This is a fact Brooks could scarcely have foreseen. The desperate need is for new concepts of exchange that will break through the ancient pattern based on the horse, the wheel, and the human back. Our technology has shattered that pattern. If we recognize this fact and take the kind of transitional steps that are necessary, then we may save what is best in our system.

Lend-lease, which was a brilliant improvisation, saved Great Britain at a moment when the total dollar balance in the British Treasury was $130,000,000. Most politicians would run in fright from the idea of peacetime lend-lease. Yet it is some such concept, under which we shall receive value, tangible or intangible, for the export of our technology, that we must discover.

To see how far advanced Brooks's ideas were for the time, we have only to realize that the debate is still going on over whether we shall or shall not intervene in world affairs. It is continuing on a level of acrimony and ignorance that gives the impresssion of a division deeper than that which exists. It goes on while the hands on the clock move forward and the little time that is left to us runs out. Because of this continuing debate, if indeed it can be dignified by the name of debate, we tend to go in both directions at once and, therefore, to expend our strength in the most futile fashion. Of Henry and Brooks it can be said that they faced the realities as they saw them and based their respective points of view on these realities. The same cannot be said of those who flee from the world of the mid-twentieth century and, fleeing, invoke the spells and totems of past superstitions.

It is small wonder, then, that the critics of 1900 dismissed *America's Economic Supremacy* with a condescending nod. The year of the turn of the century was the culmination of all human progress. We were bringing civilization to the Moros in the Philippines, having won a famous victory over the tottering empire of decadent Spain. There was not a cloud in the sky.

In a letter to Brooks in Europe, Henry in Washington referred to the reviews that were coming in, via the Romeike press clipping bureau, as "lumps of drivel." It was an accurate description. Here is one sample of the treatment accorded the new book in *Gunton's Magazine* for February 1901:

. . . Mr. Adams is a kind of fairyland philosopher. He touches facts so lightly and quickly and masses them so sweepingly as to make the solid plodding world seem in a cyclonic whirl. His style is enchanting and eloquent, his reasoning plausible, and his conclusions interestingly prophetic, but his structure is so loose and airy that it will only hold good with the aid of a most fertile imagination. He neither furnishes enough of cohesive facts or inductive reasoning to warrant the acceptance of any specific conclusion he points to. He is an excellent specimen of imaginative writers, who command the ages to obey their theories. . . . In the present work he sees England decaying and the United States destined to take its place. While the book is highly interesting reading and contains a touch-and-go reference to many important economic facts, its chief influence, so far as it exerts any, is likely to be as a contribution to a false, inflated sentiment regarding the "world destiny" of the United States, to the injury of the internal development and safeguarding of prosperity and welfare at home.

For Brooks this was a distinct retrogression. After all, Theodore Roosevelt had reviewed his *Law of Civilization and Decay* and reviewed it with considerable understanding in the *Outlook*. The ebullient Teddy had of necessity reproved Brooks for his pessimism. But still it was a provocative and stimulating book that tied together many of the leading strings of history.

Brooks was to publish two other volumes. The second of these, *The Theory of Social Revolutions*, which appeared in 1913, is in a sense a corollary of the present work. Above all it is a study of the defects in the American form of government, defects which in Brooks's view make it all but impossible to govern. Even more serious, the American form of government, as Brooks interprets it in this later work, contains inherent contradictions which, unless they are corrected, will bring down ultimate disaster. It is above all in the inflexibility of the American form of government, alongside the existence of great wealth which exerts private power but declines to accept public responsibility, that Brooks Adams sees the signals of imminent danger.

Something of this warning is implied in the present work. Brooks was deeply concerned with our capacity to take the responsibility that inevitably goes with economic power. He was acutely aware of the difficulty of reaching decisions under our system of divided authority. His studies had shown him that, in an ever more centralized world, swiftness of decision is essential above almost everything else. The American form of government seemed to him, as it did to Henry, antiquated.

In *The Theory of Social Revolutions* Brooks speaks of the fact that the ratio of man to his instruments of power had not changed essentially from the time of Alexander the Great to George Washington. The noble charter of government framed by the founding fathers, for whom Brooks had unbounded admiration, was perfectly adapted to progress in an age in which the wheel, the horse, and a low explosive were still the principal instruments of power. But Brooks pointed to the enormous changes in the ratio of power that had then come about. A horse and buggy government, as he might have expressed it, seemed to him totally inadequate in an age in which technology was making fantastic advances from year to year.

The Theory of Social Revolutions received treatment from the reviewers only a little more serious than that accorded *America's Economic Supremacy*. Here again was this professional pessimist who insisted on saying these gloomy things. He was accorded polite attention since he was an Adams, and while what he said sounded very wicked and revolutionary, that could be attributed to the New England eccentricity of all the Adams'.

The war in Europe and the growing possibility of America's involvement distracted American attention. Henry was in France when the blow fell in 1914. He and Brooks had so long anticipated doom that it could not surprise them. But it was very inconvenient and discommoding until finally the venerable Henry and his two nieces were able to get away to England. He returned to Washington for the closing years of his life. On March 27, 1918, Henry Adams died quietly in his bed without any prior illness, at the age of eighty. In Mr. Cater's collection, the last letter is from Brooks who writes to Barrett Wendell:

. . . As long as Henry lived it was the same old world. Now he is gone. Say what I will, the oldest relation in my life is closed. I, too, must go very soon, and small loss provided there be no great pain.

But there was one more service that Brooks could do for Henry out of his love and admiration. In the later years of his life Henry developed the startling theory of history first suggested in *A Letter to American Teachers of History* dated February 16, 1910. This was made more specific in "The Rule of Phase Applied to History," an essay which he sent to Brooks in manuscript form in 1912. In "The Rule of Phase" Henry employed a mathematical formula to point to the date of the doom awaiting mankind. This formula grew, in part at least, out of his knowledge of the direction in which modern physics was going. He saw that the increasing complexity and remoteness of science made for a greater and greater disparity between the ordinary level of understanding and the level of man's scientific and technical capacity, or, to phrase the last in a different way, man's capacity to destroy himself. In this disparity Henry Adams, the pessimist, saw a fatal dilemma.

Back in the old house at Quincy, in preparing his brother's last work for publication in book form, he set out to write an introduction that would show Henry's philosophy in relation to the sweep of history. But he soon found that this was too formidable a task. So, instead, Brooks wrote a kind of family chronicle that began with John Quincy Adams' troubles and ended with the renunciation by the two grandsons, Brooks and Henry, of the democratic dogma. It was not a renunciation that either had come to easily, for, as Brooks said, they had inherited it as they had inherited the family pew in the church at Quincy.

For Brooks, old and lonely, the introduction served as a summing up. It was a final warning to a curiously purblind people. In the silence of the old house, he wrote of a society in extremely unstable equilibrium, which was being attacked on every hand by potent forces from without, and which was yet being preyed on from within by a destructive tumor. That other so-called peacemaking was then in progress in Paris, and Brooks regarded it with profound doubt. Elbert H. Gary of the United States Steel Corporation had made a speech declaring that the war was the result of competition. Brooks, taking what had long been to him an obvious fact, remarked on how this matter of competition made the role of the peacemakers all but impossible. He wrote:

If the vanquished is to be conciliated, that is to say to be restored to a position in which he can act as a free man, he must be granted rights which will enable him to compete on equal terms with the victors, and the old conditions will be automatically revived. That is to say there must be a still more bitter struggle within a generation—at furthest.

He was willing to concede that the dilemma of the peacemakers was an almost insoluble one. Obviously the German people could not be destroyed as a Genghiz Khan would have destroyed them. The alternative then was to enslave them. But such a process would be far too costly to bear and, moreover, such slavery invariably degrades the enslaver.

In his last words, Brooks expressed his agreement with Henry. While the time limit in "The Rule of Phase" might not be proved accurate, the ultimate conclusion would nevertheless sooner or later be proved a certainty and "social war, or massacre, be the natural ending of the democratic philosophy," which had carried competition and the spoils system to the ultimate limit. Under the title, *The Degradation of the Democratic Dogma*, Henry Adams' last book was published in 1919, with Brooks's introduction taking 122 of the book's 317 pages.

So this Adams, with his distant and searching detachment, was through with a world that seemed bent on destroying itself. One of his preoccupations in his declining years was to prepare the house at Quincy as a public shrine. He and Henry had exchanged letters on this subject. Henry had been amused. If Brooks wanted the eighteenth century chairs he had brought from France, then he might have them to adorn his museum. It seemed to Henry a somewhat futile and foolish undertaking.

The roots of his Puritan ancestry were very deep in Brooks. An agnostic, a doubter, a profound skeptic, he returned in the last years of his life to the church at Quincy. What is more, he overcame his lifelong shyness to observe a tradition that had fallen into disuse. In the stone church at Quincy he stood up and made a public profession of his faith. Brooks Adams died on February 13, 1927.

In thus returning to the faith of his fathers, Brooks performed a symbolic act. It was an affirmative act of which Henry would have been incapable, and which underscores the difference in the world view of the two brothers. While it is true that in his last years, under the dark shadow of World War I, Brooks declared his agreement with Henry's final prescription of doom, it is also true that in his own writing he never closed the door on all hope of awakening America to a realization of her momentous destiny, a destiny already apparent on the not too distant horizon. The same thing can be said of *The Theory of Social Revolutions*. Throughout that trenchant study of social contracts and their flaws, he seems to want to warn the nation of the dangers inherent in an antiquated system of government.

At the same time, however, the determinism that was one of the chief characteristics of thought at the end of the nineteenth century runs like a strong current through all his work. The stream of determinism coming out of the last century had two branches: one was scientific, owing a great deal to Darwinism; the other was Marxist and economic. But it is quite possible that the scientific, as well as the economic, branch derives more nearly from the absolutist philosophy of

Hegel, Kant, and Fichte than we have understood. It is interesting to note Henry Adams in a letter, in the Cater collection, asking Brooks for reading references in Marx and Engels since, as he remarked sardonically, the socialist philosophy seemed likely to triumph over all others; unless, he added, it would be pure capitalism, which in the end came to the same thing.

Brooks regarded the working of economic law as inexorable. He saw no escape from the westward movement of the centers of trade, as he had described it in his most important book, even though this almost inevitably meant periodic revolution and ruin. There is no evidence to show that he was influenced by Marx, although he must have read, as Henry had, *Das Kapital*.

But the very atmosphere of Europe of the time was under the oppressive cloud of determinism. In Brooks and Henry Adams, it tended to confirm the Calvinism that came out of their New England past. Infant damnation was an important tenet in the theology of early Massachusetts. Running counter to these forces was the stout independence of character that also came out of the New England past. In Brooks's work the conflict between the iron mold of determinism and the rugged qualities of individual character is now and then apparent. His radicalism was a native product, growing out of American soil, originating in the critical quality of his mind. If it was bent in the direction of determinism, that was an influence he could scarcely have escaped.

He professed to be profoundly skeptical of human motives. In his preface to Henry's last published work, he declared that fear and greed were the forces that chiefly motivated men in their public and private actions. Obviously this contributed to his conviction of the inevitability of the doom of mankind. It was a part of his determinism and it colored what he wrote in his latter years.

In the present work, Brooks seems to take it for granted that Russia and the United States must face each other across a gulf of hostility, with conflict as the certain end. This is a disturbing attitude which we in our day must examine with honest self-searching in an effort to discover its origin. For we must frankly recognize that it is an attitude all too common today. It is expressed by Americans in high places who accept it as though in response to a dictate of which they are not consciously aware.

This unquestioning attitude is all the more disturbing when we remember how strong a factor in the Soviet mentality is the determinism that can be traced in a direct line from Hegel through Marx and Lenin. Stalin himself gave expression to it as recently as February of 1946 in the now famous campaign speech in which he said that communism and capitalism could not exist together in the same world. While Soviet apologists have said that this was merely for home consumption, the fact remains that Stalin was expressing an important tenet of Marxism which is the faith of millions of Russians and the faith, too, of millions in every other part of the world. As a religion it rejects variations of human behavior in varying systems of human society with the same ironclad predestination that marked the Calvinism of early Massachusetts.

Such a conditioning of mind, so different on the surface and yet so similar in its end result, suggests the urgent need to discover what may underlie this shared fatalism. It suggests forces at work beneath the surface of rationalization. For Freudians the theory of the deathwish is a sufficient explanation of an ailing society. But that seems scarcely more than another rationalization.

Brooks and Henry Adams were shaped by the forces that made Puritan New England, of which the Adams line was an integral part. The spectacle of the two brothers nervously examining their conviction of doom for their world is a curious and fascinating one. It is as though they were the first to succumb to a despair—a disease of despair, it might almost be called— which has in subsequent years become very widespread. We, in our time, must examine that despair courageously and objectively to determine whether or not it has grown out of a dubious science on the one hand and a false philosophy on the other.

It was understandable that Brooks in 1900 should be intensely interested in Russia. That great land mass, with its vast, inchoate people, has long exerted a fascination for the West. In 1900, as it does today, it loomed large against the Eastern horizon, troubling, mysterious, tantalizing in its Byzantine obscurity. Both Brooks and Henry had at one time or another planned to visit Russia. Unfortunately this never came about.

At the turn of the century the drive of Russian expansion was being felt throughout Asia. The ambition of the czars was not essentially different from that of the masters of the politburo, and even the technique for achieving that ambition resembles in some ways the techniques employed today. From China, sinking down into corruption and decay under the tottering regime of the Manchus, Russia had obtained permission to build a branch extending north from the Trans-Siberian Railway into Manchuria with its untapped resources. The permission specified that Russia could bring in troops to guard the new line.

Since the number of troops was not fixed, a wholesale movement of Slavs from western Russia to Asiatic Russia and Manchuria began. From the Chinese, Russia also obtained a twenty-five year lease on Port Arthur and extended its harbor and dock accommodations until it was considered one of the strongest fortresses and naval stations in Chinese waters. As many as 200,000 families are said to have been moved in the space of a few years. Then, as now, such a movement could, and did, occur without undue consideration for those who were being moved. The Trans-Siberian Railway and the movement of peoples that went along with its construction represented the kind of consolidation of the Eurasian land mass that Brooks Adams regarded as supremely significant.

Russian influence had begun to spread even into Korea, where the Russians had even constructed their own telephone line. The Russian migration began to make itself felt in the area around Peking. Every step of Russia's Asiatic advance was under constant and jealous observation by the Japanese, who saw it as a threat to their own partially formulated plans for the conquest of all of Asia.

During the Boxer Rebellion the Japanese had an opportunity to observe the conduct of Russian troops. The Russians performed very badly and the Japs began to lay their plans. Proceeding by careful and calculated design, they first built up the necessary diplomatic fences. One of the early steps was to make sure that Great Britain would regard a war against

Russia with at least benevolent neutrality. That assurance was not difficult to obtain since Russia's ambitions in Asia had long been regarded by the British as a menace to their own pre-eminent role. Japan had new cause to be alarmed when the Russians declined to withdraw the troops they had used to help put down the Boxer uprising. The Japanese Government sent repeated protests, demanding to know when Russia's forces would be removed.

When the Japanese were ready to strike, they struck as they did at Pearl Harbor, without warning. The concerted Japanese attack, skillfully planned and executed, revealed all the weaknesses in Russian organization, civil and military, that the Japanese had long known of in detail through their thorough intelligence. The Russo-Japanese war began February 8, 1904, and ended with the Treaty of Portsmouth, September 5, 1905. The Japanese had won every battle on land and sea.

In *America's Economic Supremacy* Adams had almost nothing to say about the Japanese. He apparently had no expectation of the industrial empire which Japan was to build in Manchuria. Japanese penetration was swift. Japan's industry, built around the coal and iron of Manchuria and supported by richly productive agricultural lands, became one of the chief sources of the Japanese warmaking potential after 1904. Without it the Japs could never have plotted a major war.

With the Bolshevik revolution of 1917, Japanese ambition took a new turn. In Siberia, bands of armed marauders reduced the countryside to chaos. With the end of the war in Europe in 1918, the Allies played with the idea of "putting down Bolshevism" in Russia. To help carry out this crusade the United States, in 1918, sent two regiments of troops to Vladivostok. General Graves in his revealing book, *Our Siberian Adventure*, has described this strange comedy of conflict and confusion. The Japanese were only too eager to accept the invitation of their allies to participate in the adventure. They sent in troops in far greater numbers than any other power and they showed every intention of taking permanent possession of vast areas of Asiatic Russia.

In this venture, however, they overreached themselves. A postwar scandal involving military appropriations had loud political repercussions. The Japanese militarists were temporarily checked by those who had been converted to liberal Western ideas. The Jap tide in Siberia receded, and the Soviets began to plan the industrialization of their eastern empire.

But Japan's warlords soon gained the ascendency again. The drive to industrialize Manchuria was redoubled. In 1931, by military conquest, Japan ratified an invasion that was already all but completed. The puppet state of Manchukuo was created with a puppet emperor supported by Japanese yen.

All this was swept down in World War II. In Moscow on August 14, 1945, Russia and China signed a treaty of "friendship and alliance." That treaty went a long way toward restoring the Russian position of 1900. It is a safe prediction that within a decade the Soviet Union will have absorbed a large part of Manchuria, including the richest agricultural areas.

The treaty of August 1945 creates an "exclusive naval base" at Port Arthur which "will be used only by Chinese and Soviet military and commercial vessels . . . The Chinese Government entrusts to the Soviet Government the defense of the naval base. The Soviet Government may erect at its own expense such installations as are necessary for the defense of the naval base."

The Port Arthur base, the treaty sets forth in fine style, is to be under the jurisdiction of a Sino-Soviet Military Commission. The Commission is to consist of two Chinese and three Soviet representatives. The chairman is to be appointed by the Soviets, the vice-chairman, by the Chinese. And as a supreme concession, the treaty provides that the civil administration of the area should be Chinese. It was specified that the agreement on Port Arthur should last for thirty years.

In regard to Dairen, neighboring city on the tip of

the Liao-tung Peninsula, this stragetic port on the Yellow Sea is declared by the treaty to be open to the commerce of the world. The Chinese Government agreed to lease to the U.S.S.R., free of charge, half of all the port installations and equipment. But late in 1946, Dairen was still a sealed port, and the Russsian military authorities refused permission for an American businessman and two newspapermen to disembark without word from Moscow. In March of 1947 the Soviet Government announced that Dairen would be open to the trade of the world.

The treaty also provided that the Chinese Eastern Railway and the South Manchurian Railway, from Manchouli to Suifenho and from Harbin to Dairen and Port Arthur, should be united in one under the name Chinese Chanchun Railway and operated jointly by the two countries. In that beautiful treaty language a manager was to be chosen "from among Soviet citizens" and an assistant manager, "from among Chinese citizens." The fighting along the railway, resulting in the destruction of much of it, made this section of the treaty largely inoperative.

In Russia's approach to China there is nothing new. While the methods have been somewhat more crude, it is in the pattern of the past seventy-five years. Ever since it first began to be apparent that large pieces of the loose confederation called China could be chipped away, the European powers and Japan have been doing just that.

What it comes down to is the capacity of the Chinese to administer efficiently the government of a vast domain. There is no sign that they will acquire that capacity in the near future. In fact all the signs point in the opposite direction. That is one of the reasons why it will be relatively simple for the Soviet Union to consolidate, economically and culturally first and then perhaps politically, a large part of Manchuria. The techniques that Russia employs today are far more effective than those of 1900.

North Manchuria is flanked by the new industrial empire that the U.S.S.R. has created in Siberia. In a remarkably short time, major industries have come into being in this remote part of the world. When Henry Wallace and his party visited Siberia in the spring of 1944, they witnessed the launching of an eight thousand ton ocean-going vessel at Komsomolsk on the Amur River. Not until 1932 did the first four thousand members of the Komsomolsk, or Young Communist League, initiate this settlement on a strategic site on the Amur. Today it has an estimated population of one hundred thousand. Komsomolsk is only one of a number of industrial centers that have sprung up at the bidding of the planners in the Kremlin.

The network of modern railways in Siberia is being

constantly expanded. The latest addition is the Southern Trans-Siberian Railway connecting Kuznetsk in
Siberia with Kuibyshev on the Volga. The *Bolshevik*,
the authoritative journal of the politburo, gave a per-
centage table showing how the East is rapidly catching
up to the West in industrial potential. The table compares the share of industrial production coming out of
Siberia in 1940 and the share that is estimated from the
East for 1950:

	1940	1950
	Per Cent	Per Cent
Iron Ore	29	44
Steel	34	51
Rolled Steel	33	51
Coal	36	47.5
Oil	12	36

One weakness, however, is that food must be
brought from western Russia, and since the distance
is so great, it is a severe handicap. But now the rich
food-producing areas of Manchuria will be made a
part of this industrial complex. From these same areas
Japan obtained vast supplies of grain, soy beans, and
fertilizer. The farmers of Manchuria will be able to
obtain manufactured goods from Siberia in return for
their produce.

This new industry has sent a quickening current
throughout all of Asia. The example of what the

U.S.S.R. has done to raise the living standards and the status of ancient and long-submerged peoples, such as the Yakuts, is propaganda of a far more powerful nature than any persuasion on the radio or in print. The propaganda of example was important in the Soviet penetration of Outer Mongolia. One of the clauses of the Sino-Soviet treaty of August 1945, granted the people of Outer Mongolia their independence "should a plebiscite . . . confirm this desire." This great expanse of territory, so strategically placed with respect to Manchuria, is, in effect, one of the states of the Soviet Union. In the exchange of notes on Outer Mongolia incorporated in the treaty, V. M. Molotov stated that his government would "respect the political independence and territorial integrity of the People's Republic of Mongolia."

Russia's action in stripping the Japanese industrial plant in Manchuria has been given great emphasis in the press in America. How much direct benefit this was to the Soviet Union is a question. The United States reparations' representative, Edwin W. Pauley, put a value of roughly $800,000,000 on the machinery the Russians carted off. The Russians themselves set the amount at $95,000,000. It is quite possible that the damage done to industry in Manchuria approximated the Pauley figure. But it is also possible that the value of the Russian loot, once it had been torn out of its base, was not very much greater than the estimate given by the Soviets. The important thing, and it may have been the chief objective of the Russian armies, is that the productive capacity of Manchuria has been destroyed. Unless, and until, it is rebuilt, it cannot serve as the base for an attack against Soviet Siberia.

While earth-shaking events intervened in the nearly fifty years that have elapsed, it nevertheless seems that the destiny which Brooks Adams foresaw for Russia in Asia is to be realized. When all the factors are weighed, the position of the Soviets in 1947 appears to be well advanced over that of the czar in 1900. Japan, a dangerous rival, lies in ruins, confined to the narrow compass of her islands. Korea is flanked and on the way to being sovietized under the repressive policy of the occupation in the Soviet zone and is likely to fall entirely under Russian domination. The strategic ports are again in the control of Russia. The Kuriles and all of the island of Sakhalin are once more Russian possessions. China seems hopelessly weak and divided with the Chinese Communists closely allied to the Soviet Union.

What is, perhaps, most important of all is that the industry that has been built up in Asiatic Russia is far more strategically located, remote from attack, than it would have been if the development of 1900 had continued without interruption. Thus, the consolidation of the Eurasian land mass which Brooks Adams foresaw is coming about in a way that he could scarcely have anticipated. As a counterpoise, we hold the islands of the Pacific, which is fitting, since, in comparative terms at any rate, we are a naval rather than a land power. But it must not be forgotten that these are unproductive possessions which we must maintain at great cost.

With respect to Great Britain, Brooks will be accused by some of prejudice. It is a prejudice that might almost be called a family inheritance. Out of his bitter experience in England during our Civil War, Henry had this family trait in a highly developed form. But it should be added that Henry's prejudices were so extensive that they covered human beings of almost every class and category.

Brooks was more tolerant. He recognized the role that Great Britain had played for nearly a century in keeping order in the world. What is more, he recognized the fact that America had consistently relied on that power. The whole basis of American foreign policy, as formulated in the Monroe Doctrine, was predicated on British dominance in the Atlantic and on the police power that she exercised over all the sea lanes. During the Spanish-American War, England checkmated Germany's half-veiled intention of exploiting that crisis.

This book is devoted in considerable part to analyzing the reasons why Great Britain was being forced to surrender her dominant position. It was published a year before death ended the reign of Queen Victoria, which exceeded in length that of any other British monarch. England's power seemed entrenched in every corner of the earth. In the autobiography of his early life, *A Roving Commission*, Winston Churchill gives an unforgettable picture of the golden years that came at the end of the nineteenth century. Those in positions of power and prestige felt themselves the masters of a destiny that had no date. But as Brooks Adams, the skeptical New Englander, was quick to discover, the golden glow in the sky was a sunset glow. The base of the economic structure was deeply flawed. Those flaws, in terms of balance of payments, the movement of gold, and so on, were susceptible to the kind of measurement that Brooks understood.

In the light of what is happening today, we can see how traditional ways of thinking obscured the true meaning of events after 1900. Britain's position after the turn of the century grew steadily worse. It was increasingly difficult for her to meet the competition of

Germany on the one hand and the United States on the other. In 1914 the competition with Germany passed into the shooting stage. It was necessary for Britain to turn almost at once to the United States for large loans, which were to come from the money center in New York. After 1917 loans and large supplies of food and munitions were furnished by the Government in Washington.

During World War I, Great Britain obtained $4,074,800,000 from the United States in loans which were never repaid. Without those grants she would have been nearly as badly off in 1919 as in 1947. British pride and arrogance on the one hand and the traditional attitudes of Americans toward Britain's power on the other hand made it impossible to get a realistic understanding of what was actually happening.

During World War I, France obtained $3,340,500,000, which was in effect a grant that sustained the French through an ordeal that at least twice brought them to the verge of defeat. It may be possible to debate whether American military aid tipped the scales in favor of the victory of November 1918. But there is no room for debate over the influence of American dollars and American supplies. They saved the economic structure of Great Britain and western Europe. And because that precarious structure was temporarily saved, there was the illusion that nothing essential had been changed. Or it might be more accurate to say that we carefully cherished that illusion. Beneath the outward surface of things-as-they-were in France, a deep divisiveness was at work. It went along with the symptoms of bankruptcy, financial and political, that were all too evident below the surface. The end was the debacle of 1940. Today, France is being pulled apart by the pulls from West and East.

During the 'twenties the dubious structure of western Europe was further sustained by the system of reparation loans to Germany from America. About $208,250,000 were pumped into the Weimar Republic from the New York money center. It was the oxygen which kept the feeble republic alive while the forces of extreme right and left were growing stronger. At the same time, a part of this money was pumped out of Germany as reparations, thereby helping France and England to maintain a temporary equilibrium.

It has now become obvious what the system of war and reparation loans really was. It was an elaborate subterfuge which made it possible for America to exercise some degree of the economic supremacy that was ours, while at the same time preserving the deception that our interest in Europe and the rest of the world was merely that of benevolent detachment. This elaborate pretense was like a curtain we put up to screen from our unwilling eyes the realities of our new position. Behind that curtain we tried to live in self-satisfied isolation.

This reaction was understandable. Everything in our history had contributed to the conviction that we were a continent sufficient unto ourselves. Behind the bulwark of British sea power, we advanced to the western shore of the Pacific. In the reaches of this continent, with its great range of climate, there was almost everything we needed to prosper and grow great. Exploiting the resources of forest, mine, and stream, we developed wealth on a scale that the world had never seen before, and the opportunities for the ordinary citizen were such as to create a legend of hope wherever men sweated and toiled in hopelessness.

Completely absorbed in our conviction of self-sufficiency, we failed to comprehend the meaning of two phenomena. The first was the decline and the threatening bankruptcy of Great Britain. The second was the centralizing force of the new technology rapidly pushing back the ocean barriers and reducing the world to a scale unbelievably small. Brooks and Henry Adams could cross the ocean in a fraction of the time that it took their grandfather to go from Quincy to Washington.

We were not alone, of course, in our determined effort to preserve the illusion of a past that had all but completely vanished. England in the 'thirties played the role of a wayward ostrich. Historians in the future will have great difficulty in understanding the willful blindness of the democracies.

What happened in the spring of 1940 wakened many Americans out of their long dream of insular isolation. With western Europe occupied by the Germans, it seemed suddenly as though one whole side of the world had fallen away, leaving a void that was full of dark uncertainty. Russia and Germany were linked by the pact of August 1939. It hardly seemed possible that the British, beleaguered on their little island, could stand.

Yet so deeply rooted were the habits of thought growing out of our continental self-sufficiency that a large proportion of the public remained indifferent or hostile to the idea of anything that would involve us in what was said to be a foreign quarrel. Many of our leaders knew how the Nazi victory had imperiled America. General George C. Marshall, who had a clear understanding of the extent of the German objective, which was not less than world conquest, tried frantically to stir Congress to the need of adopting elementary measures of security. The margin of his success, as in the vote on the continuation of the draft in the fall of 1940, was often painfully small.

In order to help Britain, which Brooks Adams in

1900 had called the "fortified outpost of the Anglo-Saxon world," it was necessary again to resort to subterfuge. President Roosevelt introduced the device of lend-lease to send to England the aid that might sustain her. The debate on the Lend-Lease Act in the Senate early in 1941 had at times a quality of pure fantasy as those who championed it argued that by such measures we could avoid involvement in Europe's quarrel. There was, however, a realization that the decision meant more than the proponents of the act would or could admit.

There had been earlier steps leading up to lend-lease. Late in 1939 the Embargo Act was repealed, thereby permitting the shipment of war matériel to the Allies. I well remember the day on which the late Senator William E. Borah stood up as the gloomy light of a November afternoon filtered into the chamber and declaimed what we all knew was his valedictory. The old man in a feeble, almost inaudible voice uttered the protest of isolationist America.

But still the approach was that of subterfuge. Even eager volunteers felt the necessity of deception, or self-deception, in view of the stubborn determination of so many Americans to live in the past. The very name, Committee to Defend America by Aiding the Allies, was a recognition of this necessity. It was a surreptitious back door through which we proposed to enter the struggle if, indeed, we entered it at all.

Americans who went overseas in World War II learned the terrors of modern warfare at first hand. They saw cities reduced to rubble and whole populations driven to living like animals under the ground. They learned the meaning of the overpowering speed of the modern bomber and the guided missile falling through the stratosphere faster than sound. But for most Americans, taking it at second hand, the war had an unreality, as though it were occurring on another planet. For many it meant greater prosperity than they had ever known.

This helps to explain the drive to get back to normal that began on the day the war ended. In our headlong haste, we invited a dangerous degree of inflation that might have been prevented if we had been willing for a little while longer to submit to the discipline of war. A boom swept the nation. Outwardly, the pattern was the same. After prolonged maneuvering and debate, the Senate approved a loan to Great Britain of $3,500,000,000 by a vote of forty-six to thirty-four. We preached to the British about their conduct in India and Palestine.

Then early in 1947 the desperate plight of Britain became so apparent that we could no longer ignore what it meant. Sidney Campbell, the financial editor of Reuter's, in an article in *The New York Times* predicted bankruptcy and collapse unless England was somehow able to adjust her balance of payments on more favorable terms. The threatening crisis was compared with that which followed the fall of Constantinople in the fifteenth century. The note to Washington on Greece soon followed. Britain could not sustain her commitments around the world. The total in all branches of Britain's armed services was about a million and a half. Gloomy members of the Attlee Government were insisting that this was far beyond Britain's means and would have to be cut in half. There were reports of an ominous black market in pounds.

In the summer of 1947 the drain on the British loan was far greater than had been anticipated. Nearly $2,000,000,000 of the $3,750,000,000 which was made available for a period of five and a half years had been used. The rate of withdrawals had risen steeply and the more pessimistic prophets believed that in another year the total would be exhausted. In the face of an unfavorable trade balance running at the rate of nearly two billion dollars a year, the British were trying manfully to prevent bankruptcy. World War II had wiped out the last bulwark of external capital which had helped in the years between the wars to keep the deficits from becoming catastrophic. Britain had not merely cashed in external capital assets of about £1,-200,000,000, but she had increased her external debts by £3,000,000,000.

When it is set against this background, the full significance of President Truman's message on aid to Greece is seen. The inexorable pressure of circumstances had at last compelled an American president to intervene directly in America's interest in a dispute five thousand miles away. In Congress and throughout the country, too, this fact in all its stark significance produced a kind of shock which was compounded of bewilderment and resentment. The British barrier was down; the barrier taken for granted so long that many Americans preferred to believe it had never been there at all.

As this is written, Congress is moving toward a decision. Even those who have persisted in blind isolationism seem to be accepting the necessity of action, although with a kind of churlish reluctance. The alternative is so plain. It is to spend our accumulated resources in a few years of good living while the world around us is reshaped in such a way that our existence as a free people eventually will not be possible. We cannot long evade the responsibility that is an inherent part of our power.

There are great dangers in the course on which we are now setting out. We are making a late start. In the words that General Marshall once used about the dilemma of his own position when he became Secretary of State, it is "a desperate adventure against time." Our Rip van Winkle sleep lasted so long. We are still resentful of being wakened. More than anything else we would like to return to the blissful state of innocence and ignorance we enjoyed until the hammer blows on the door could not be ignored. An editorial that appeared in the *Economist* as the implications of the Truman Doctrine were being debated posed the question. Entitled "Imperialism or Indifference?" it said:

. . . If raw material resources, industrial capacity, scientific knowledge, productive "know-how," skilled labor —if these alone were the ingredients of power, then the United States could take on the rest of the world single-handed. But though these things are essential ingredients, they are not all that it takes to make a Great Power. There must also be the willingness, and the ability, to use economic resources in support of national policy. The rulers of Soviet Russia . . . are not likely, at least for a generation to come, to have nearly as good cards in their hands as the Americans. But the nature of their system of concentrated power and iron censorship enables them to play a forcing game. The Americans' hand is all trumps; but will any of them ever be played? And for what purpose?

One danger is that in our new-found resolution, if it is indeed a resolution, we shall sweep down the first frail beginnings of international co-operation through the United Nations. This was a profound misgiving in the hearts of many who heard the President's appeal. He seemed to ignore the machinery of the United Nations available to check the dissolution and decay in Greece. The fact is, however, that the United Nations is itself so divided by the controversy between Russia and the West that effective action in the instance of Greece would have been all but impossible. The Security Council sent a United Nations commission to Greece to investigate border incidents. The reports of what the Slav members of that commission saw and heard were diametrically opposed to the reports of what the representatives of Britain, France, and the United States saw and heard. A commission that cannot agree on ordinary facts could hardly agree on a solution for the political-economic tangle in Greece.

We have a right, however, to hope that once American missions have taken the first steps, there will be an opportunity to call on specialized units of the United Nations. Thus, the Food and Agricultural Organization completed an invaluable survey of Greek needs and at the same time outlined a program for rehabilitation.

But the question of real moment concerns our capacity to act. The role of guide, counselor, policeman, is so utterly alien. For the most part we have approached the world beyond our shores with the tourist mentality; a simple curiosity about what was foreign and strange; a condescending good will coupled with a supreme assurance that our way of life was the only way of life. This was the American attitude. The expatriates were those who could not accept the American pattern. So few of us are prepared to take responsibility in distant parts of the earth.

This is a handicap which could be overcome. Far more serious are the difficulties inherent in our system of government with its divided powers. Our antiquated government was a source of deep concern to Brooks Adams who foresaw the test to which it would be put. The power of steam was an enormously centralizing force, as Brooks understood. Yet our form of government remained unchanged. In the age of mass power, its anomalies and contradictions were such as to threaten imminent breakdown, or so Brooks saw it in *The Theory of Social Revolutions*.

We in our time see how nearly impossible it is to reach a decision when the authority of government is divided between the opposing parties. And that has happened under our system on the average of one out of every three years. In an earlier day the consequences were not too serious. The major decisions were made in the money centers in London and New York. Behind the great barrier of the seas we had little to fear.

The problem of governing under our system is now more acute than ever. The postwar readjustment was complicated and confused by the fact that a coalition of Republicans and Democrats opposed the Democratic President on most issues. After November 5, 1946, we had a Democrat in the White House and Republican majorities in both houses of Congress. In the past that has meant stalemate. What we have today is close to stalemate.

Traditionally, this division has coincided with an interval of pause in which both parties prepare for the next presidential election. But today, that interval can have the most fateful and far-reaching consequences. Such a gulf of suspicion and rivalry divides the two branches of government that even routine functions are endlessly delayed. Thus, for months on end the atomic energy project was immobilized while Congress quarreled over the appointments made by the President. In such a condition of paralysis, able men are reluctant to accept Government appointment. And if they have ever held any original ideas or done any bold thinking, they are promptly suspect.

On the part of some there seemed to be a desire to put a stigma on Government service. In one of the last essays he wrote, Brooks Adams commented grimly on the fact that government in America was perforce content with second- or third-rate brains. It seemed to him a tragic perversion of the whole concept of patriotism and the common good that the ablest men should reject public service for private endeavor and their personal fortunes. He saw in it a warning sign of deterioration and decline.

While the dilemma of government by division should be glaringly apparent, there is little indication of a concern over this basic fault. After the election of November 1946, Senator William Fulbright of Arkansas tried to dramatize the impending stalemate by suggesting that the President resign to be succeeded by a Republican in order that there might be unity. This suggestion was treated as a kind of impertinence; a reflection on Mr. Truman's fortitude.

The crisis over Greece is a perfect illustration of the need for quick decision. On February 24, a British note informed the United States that Great Britain could furnish no economic assistance to Greece after March 31. For a long time there had been persistent hints of this. The Greek fiscal year ends on March 31. The Government in Athens was so weak that it could not long endure without at least the assurance of help. Withdrawal of the British troops in August was still another imminent deadline to be met.

Here was a matter requiring urgent action by a Government capable of taking a sure, swift decision and then carrying it out. Under our system of divided authority, the Democratic President went to the Republican Congress with his request. Inevitably it was given a political coloration. To grant the request would be to do a favor to a political rival. The system itself conditions that attitude. The result is endless and repetitive inquiry followed by prolonged debate. When the move is finally made, if it is made, a large part of its value will have been destroyed by the delay and the controversy.

A study of events during the past decade indicates that because decisions are constantly postponed for lack of co-ordinated authority, we are forever blundering into crises. Because we cannot resolve the minor crisis, action is postponed and postponed and postponed until we find ourselves in a major crisis or, that is to say, in a war.

Greece is again an illustration. A positive policy for Greece and the Middle East should have been shaped immediately after V-J Day. The fact of our economic and technological power made it obvious that we were the only nation capable of furnishing the money, the machines, and the technicians to help the poverty-ridden peoples of the Middle East. If this could have been done through the United Nations, so much the better. But here was a great vacuum of need that sooner or later would have to be filled. To wait until a crisis forced some action was to wait until it was very nearly too late.

In the Soviet Union the decisions are made by a very few men. While it may be an oversimplification to say they are made by a single dictator, this is at least approximately true. It makes for certainty of decision. But, as under all dictatorships, it also makes for inefficiency in the execution of those decisions; for fear, insecurity, delay, sterility, complete lack of initiative, and the suppression of all imagination; for a cumbersome and deadening bureaucracy that throttles all of life.

In Russia, this is a very old story as we know from Gogol. It is possible, however, that the weight of the bureaucracy today is greater and more oppressive than it has ever been. Even the most minor decisions are passed along to the very top level, with interminable delays as a consequence.

Looking at this example of a bureaucracy under dictatorship, we can feel that our own system is infinitely superior. But if we will look objectively at the real relationship between the U. S. A. and the U.S.S.R., considered as rivals with rival systems, we shall soon see that this is not the moment to be complacent. We must understand that today we are an island and as an island we confront the great Eurasian land mass which Russia seeks to consolidate under a single authority situated in Moscow.

It is this relationship that Brooks Adams perceived. We are dependent upon the sea lanes and the air lanes. Of necessity we must develop the capacity and the skills to keep the lines of communication and trade open. Russian inefficiency, Russian provincialism, Russian mistakes are compensated for by the vast expanse of territory from Vladivostok and Port Arthur to its western border. They are compensated for, too, by the amazing stamina and virility of 180,000,000 Russians. Here is a margin for error, a margin such as we once had but which we have no longer. Soviet industry has been dispersed, thanks in part to the pressures of the recent war. Behind the Urals and in Siberia a new industry has come into being, the extent of which can only be guessed at. Even against atomic weapons Russia has an enormous advantage in mass and distance.

How far the limits of the Soviet Empire will extend in the West is still a question. It is possible to see in Russia's approach to conquered Germany a concerted and carefully considered plan to bring that defeated nation within the Russian periphery. That was the charge made as the foreign ministers began their second postwar conference in Moscow. Behind the demand for unification, those who believe in the ever pressing force of Russian expansionism could see a Soviet plan to communize all of Germany as the population in the Soviet zone has been communized. At stake, too, was the Ruhr with its vast industrial potential.

One thing we do know: that is, how little we really know about the German-Russian relationship since 1917. Lenin spoke of Germany as "the principal link in the chain of revolutions." After 1918 both Russia and Germany were under the ban. This gave them a bond which led to the training of Germany's military technicians and airmen in the Soviet Union in order to circumvent the Versailles Treaty. German officers, to return the favor, helped shape the Red Army.

The Soviet purge of 1937 and after may or may not have been directed at Russian officers suspected of being under the influence of the Nazis. There are those who contend that its objective was exactly the opposite: to remove the old Bolsheviks who would never sanction a treaty with Fascist Germany. Certainly most of the old Bolsheviks were eliminated. And we must add, as a kind of footnote, the curious fact that in spite of repeated warnings from both London and Washington, the masters of the Kremlin refused to believe that Germany intended to attack the Soviet Union. Even the approximate date of the attack was furnished, and yet, when it came, the advantage of surprise was all with the Nazis.

These are details that may ultimately be fitted into the broad generalization of history which was Brooks Adams' achievement. From *America's Economic Supremacy* we have much to learn. We can believe in, and hope and work for, international co-operation and world government which will mean the end of rival sovereignties. But we cannot afford to ignore the inexorable movement of the lines of force and power. Tracing these relationships, Brooks looked beyond the surface beliefs of his day. He was not afraid to challenge the unthinking optimism that was like an all-encompassing rainbow across the American sky at the end of the last century.

To believe in that rainbow and its perpetual promise was an article of faith. He disbelieved out of the deep intellectual and moral questioning that was a part of his New England inheritance. And he set down his disbeliefs, which were also, if one examines them closely, his beliefs. They were not the easy beliefs of his day. The hope and the promise were still there, as they had been in the time of John Adams and John Quincy Adams, although now the tenure of the hope was brief. In the view of this prophetic Puritan, payment on the promise would not be handed down from heaven as our divine right. It would come to us if we understood, if we accepted the duties as well as the rights that go with power.

APRIL 1947

SOMERSET, MARYLAND

AMERICA'S
ECONOMIC SUPREMACY

The Spanish War and the Equilibrium of the World

COULD we regard the Spanish War as calmly as if it were a thing of the past, we should doubtless perceive that it formed a link in a long chain of events which, when complete, would represent one of those memorable revolutions wherein civilizations pass from an old to a new condition of equilibrium. The last such revolution ended with Waterloo; the one now at hand promises to be equally momentous.

In 1760 Holland, probably, still contained the economic center of the civilized world; but by 1815 that center had indisputably moved northwest to the mouth of the Thames. England had become the focus of capital and industry, and second to England—and to England alone—stood France. It then appeared as though the seat of empire had definitely established itself in the region of Europe contained between the Atlantic Ocean, the North Sea, and the Rhine; but, on looking back, the inference is unavoidable that decay must have set in almost at once; for in 1870 France, after a sharp struggle, collapsed. Since 1870 the forces which caused this catastrophe have continued to operate with increased energy.

The conclusion to be drawn from these premises is that, from either a military or an economic standpoint, the equilibrium of 1815 has been destroyed. Disintegration seems to have set in; and that disintegration is sweeping capital and industry in opposite directions from their former centers—to the east from Paris, and to the west from London. On the Continent the focus of industry has long since crossed the Rhine, and is receding toward the Vistula; while an equally marked tide has run from the British Isles toward America.

Perhaps the simplest illustration of this phenomenon is the iron trade, the basis of modern manufactures. In the middle of the last century, France led in the production of pig iron; England and Germany were nearly equal; while America produced but little. The pig iron produced in 1740 was as follows: France, 26,000 tons; Great Britain, 20,000; Germany, 18,000; America, 1,000 tons.

During the next hundred years England distanced France; France gained relatively on Germany; and America increased her product from one-twentieth to more than one-fifth of that of the United Kingdom.

The following was the production of pig iron in 1840: Great Britain, 1,390,000 tons; France, 350,000; United States, 290,000; Germany, 170,000 tons.

After 1870 the movement became accelerated. Between 1880 and 1896 the German output grew from 2,729,038 to 6,360,982 tons; while that of France, which had been 1,725,293 tons in 1880, was only 2,333,702 in 1896. The following extract from the *Industrial World* of February 3, 1898, puts in a nutshell the altered relations of the two nations:

The rapidity with which the manufacture of hardware has grown in Germany may be judged from the fact that it compared with that of France in 1875 as four to three, and in 1895 as five to two.

But if Germany has outstripped France, the activity of America has been even greater. In 1840 the United States had not entered the field of international competition; in 1897 she undersold the English in London; and her product for 1898 promises nearly to equal that of Great Britain and France combined.

In Great Britain the production of pig iron in 1880 was 7,749,233 tons; in 1896, 8,660,000; and in 1897, about 8,930,000 tons. Her exports of the same were: in 1880, 1,632,343 tons; in 1896, 1,060,165; and in 1897, 1,201,104 tons. Thus it would appear that the English iron industry is relatively stationary.

The United States, on the other hand, in 1870 produced 1,665,179 tons of pig iron; in 1880, 3,840,000; and in 1897, 9,807,123 tons; while for the present year the estimates reach a million tons a month. (The actual production for 1898 was 11,962,317 tons.)

The exports of pig iron amounted last year to 600-000 tons; and manufactured steel is exported in increasing quantities not only to India, Australia, Japan, and Russia, but to the United Kingdom itself. As the *Economist* of April 16, 1898, observed:

The fact, that the United States is now able to produce pig-iron and some forms of steel cheaper than this country, is a serious menace to our foreign trade in the future.

Furthermore, there are indications that accumulated wealth is following in the track of industry. With France this proposition seems demonstrable. The outflow began with the war indemnity of 1871, which, alone, may have tipped the balance toward Germany; and since 1870 the victors have continually squeezed the vanquished. Isolated and weak, France, with the instinct of self-preservation, has amalgamated with Russia, and, to strengthen her ally, has remitted thither the bullion which might have expanded her manufactures at home. The amount lent has been estimated at $2,000,000,000—perhaps it is more. Certainly it has sufficed to vitalize northern Asia. Under this impulsion the Russian empire has solidified, and mills and workshops have sprung up on the southern Steppes; while Poland is becoming a manufacturing province. The Russian railway system is stretching eastward; it is under construction to Peking; and it is said to be projected to Hankow, the commercial capital of the great central provinces of China. Nor has Russia alone benefited. No small portion of this great sum has percolated to Germany, where the Russians have bought because of advantageous prices. Thus, yielding to a resistless impulsion, France is being drawn into the vortex of a Continental system whose center travels eastward.

The United Kingdom, though untouched by war, has presented nearly parallel phenomena. The weak spot of English civilization is the failure of the Kingdom to feed the people. This failure not only necessitates a regularly increasing outlay but throws the nation on an external base in case of war. A comparison of quinquennial averages, taken at equal periods since 1870, shows that, while the value of exports has regularly fallen, the value of imports has risen, until the discrepancy has become enormous; the growth of the adverse balance in twenty-five years having been 20 per cent. The following table will explain the situation:

EXPORTS AND IMPORTS OF THE UNITED KINGDOM

Total Exports

Periods	Amounts	Decrease
1871–1875	£1,197,512,196	
1881–1885	1,161,429,669	3%
1891–1895	1,134,770,481	2⅓%

Total Imports Less Re-exports

Periods	Amounts	Increase
1871–1875	£1,510,099,864	
1881–1885	1,682,727,419	11%
1891–1895	1,775,694,339	5½%

Last year the apparent deficit reached £157,055-000 (nearly $800,000,000); and the first four months of 1898 show a loss of £10,000,000, as compared with the same months of 1897. (The adverse balance in 1898 reached £176,594,207.) Nor does the mere statement of the figures reveal the gravity of the situation. The effect is cumulative; for as charges grow, surplus income declines. However large a revenue the British may have drawn from foreign investments when those investments were in their prime, no one supposed it to be £160,000,000; and there can be no doubt that their income from this source has shrunk considerably. First, the interest rate is less than formerly; second, bankruptcy has wiped out many debts since 1890; third, there has been a heavy sale of foreign—especially American—securities in London. Yet, in spite of such sales, many millions of gold have been shipped lately to New York; and bankers believe that many millions more are loaned in London at higher interest than can be obtained here. Most significant of all, perhaps, is the fact that Sir James Westland, the Indian Minister of Finance, inclines to ascribe the crises in Hindustan rather to the withdrawal of English funds than to the closing of the mints. These facts tend to show not only that Great Britain is spending her capital but that the flow of her money is toward America, as the flow from France is across the Rhine. Englishmen, it is true, having regard for the growth of their revenue, consider themselves most prosperous. They certainly enjoy a large surplus; and yet, perhaps, this elasticity is hardly reassuring. On analysis, the items of taxation which show the chief increase are the succession duties and the excise. The one is notoriously a socialistic measure; while the other indicates increased extravagance in drink.

Turning from the economic to the military standpoint, the altered attitude of Europe is at least equally impressive. Lord Salisbury once described the disease which devoured the Balkan country as "gangrene." The same gangrene is devouring all the Latin races. The aggressive energy of France is, perhaps, dead. Few now believe her able, singlehanded, to withstand Germany; and this feebleness draws her toward that social system which promises at no very distant day to consolidate northern Europe and Asia in a mass hostile to the interests of all external races. Such a consolidation, should it mature, must threaten not the prosperity only, but the very existence, of England. Should it prevail, her geographical position would become hopelessly eccentric, and she would also be thrown upon the United States for food. At present there are but two localities where the wants of the British people can be certainly supplied: one is the coast of the Black Sea, the other that of North America. Under such conditions, however, the Black Sea would lie in the enemy's power; while the United States could probably close the St. Lawrence as well as her own ports. The support of the United States may thus be said to be vital to England, since, without it, if attacked by a Continental coalition, she would have to capitulate. Great Britain may, therefore, be not inaptly described as a fortified outpost of the Anglo-Saxon race, overlooking the eastern continent and resting upon America. Each year her isolation grows more pronounced;

and, as it grows, the combination against her assumes more and more the character of Napoleon's method of assault, which aimed to subdue an insular and maritime antagonist by controlling the coasts whence that antagonist drew its subsistence.

Unconsciously, perhaps, to herself, insecurity as to her base has warped every movement of England and has given to her foreign policy the vacillation which has lately characterized it. This weakness has caused her to abandon Port Arthur, to permit Germany to occupy Kiao Chou, and to look with pleasure to an alliance with this country.

But, if the United States is essential to England, England is essential to the United States, in the face of the enemies who fear and hate us, and who, but for her, would already have fleets upon our shores. More than this, the prosperity of England is our prosperity. England is our best, almost our only certain market. She is the chief vent for our surplus production; and anything which cripples her purchasing power must react on us. For years past she has been losing her commanding industrial position. Her most lucrative trade today lies with the Far East; and if she is shut out there, her resources will be seriously impaired, and the money she no longer earns cannot be spent for food. Moreover, in those regions the interests of the two peoples are identical. The Russians hardly veil their purpose of reversing, by means of railways, the current of the Chinese trade as it has flowed for ages, and of using force to discriminate against maritime nations; but those who are excluded from the Eastern trade have always lagged behind in the race for life. Approached thus, the problems presented by the Spanish War become defined. Competition has entered a period of greater stress; and competition, in its acutest form, is war. The present outbreak is, probably, only premonitory; but the prize at stake is now what it has always been in such epochs, the seat of commercial exchanges—in other words, the seat of empire. For upward of a thousand years the social center of civilization has advanced steadily westward. Should it continue to advance, it will presently cross the Atlantic and aggrandize America. If, on the contrary, it should recede, America may have reached her prime. In the future the conflict will apparently lie—as it has done in the past—between the maritime and the unmaritime races, or between the rival merits of land and sea transport. A glance at history will prove the antiquity and fierceness of this strife.

From the earliest times, China and India seem to have served as the bases of human commerce; the seat of empire having always been the point where their products have been exchanged against the products of the West. In the dawn of civilization, this point vibrated between Chaldea and Assyria; Babylon or Nineveh being the metropolis, as one or the other gained possession of the wholesale trade. The Phoenicians, on the coast, acted as carriers; and through them the shores of the Mediterranean were developed. As this development went on, the focus of affairs advanced to Carthage; and when Rome destroyed Carthage, exchanges passed from Africa to Italy, and the ancient civilization rapidly culminated. The law may, perhaps, be stated somewhat thus: In proportion as the Western races acquire the capacity for consuming Eastern products, the sphere of civilization expands, and the energy of centralization increases. Conversely, in proportion as the West has either lain dormant, or has lost the power of consumption, civilization has receded into Asia, and has there, in the valley of the Euphrates and the Tigris, created capitals, of which Nineveh, Babylon, and Bagdad may be taken as types.

Following this law, from the fourth century onward, as Italy, Gaul, and Spain sank into barbarism, and Byzantium herself came to resemble a fortified frontier post, peddling at retail to hunters and shepherds, the wholesale trade receded to Ctesiphon, on the Tigris, where in the early part of the seventh century, reigned Chosroes, the greatest of potentates. At this time the Eastern Empire reached its lowest ebb. Poverty paralyzed the Greek armies. Constantinople

built no churches, erected no statues, illuminated no
books, neglected her coinage, and forgot her arts. In
618 the Emperor Heraclius, a great soldier, so de-
spaired, that he freighted a fleet with his treasures, and
prepared for a flight to Africa. At this moment of
utter exhaustion on the Bosphorus, Gibbon has thus
described the magnificence of Dastagerd, in the valley of the Tigris, the abode of the Persian king:

Six thousand guards successively mounted before the
palace-gate; the service of the interior apartments was performed by twelve thousand slaves. . . . The various
treasures of gold, silver, gems, silk, and aromatics were
deposited in a hundred subterraneous vaults. . . . The
voice of flattery, and perhaps of fiction, is not ashamed
to compute the thirty thousand rich hangings that
adorned the walls; the forty thousand columns of silver,
or more probably of marble and plated wood, that supported the roof; and the thousand globes of gold sus-
pended in the dome, to imitate the motions of the planets
and the constellations of the zodiac.

The peculiarity of the path of exchanges is that it
lies east and west, not north and south. When Byzantium lost her Western market, the possession of Egypt
or North Africa availed little. She became poor; and,
as usual, poverty reacted on itself. The Greeks failed
to protect their communications with Central Asia;
Chosroes first succeeded in blocking the caravan

routes, and then in invading Syria and Egypt and occupying their ports. When he had thus isolated his
enemy, he had no difficulty in keeping an army at Chal-
cedon for ten years, in sight of St. Sophia. Had the
Persians then commanded the sea, they would surely
have succeeded where Artaxerxes had failed centuries
before at Salamis. Certainly in the reign of Heraclius
the Greeks were harder pressed than in the time of
Themistocles; and would in any event almost inevitably have succumbed to the blockade had it not been
for the advent of the Saracens. The Hegira occurred
in 622; and the diversion was decisive. In 637 the Mos-
lems sacked Ctesiphon, the Persian Empire crumbled,
the ancient avenues of traffic were reopened, and exchanges began that long journey westward which has
lasted till today. Constantinople was the first point in
Europe to feel the impulsion. Her energy returned
with her commerce; and by the ninth century she was
again the seat of wealth and empire. Nevertheless her
prosperity was ephemeral; fluctuating with that sen-
sitive equilibrium which is the sport of war.

In the tenth century, as in the days of Nebuchad-
nezzar, the usual route from the Orient to the West
lay up the Persian Gulf and the Euphrates to Thap-
sacus, and across Syria by caravan; with the difference
that it reached the sea by Aleppo and Antioch instead
of by Tyre or Sidon.

Accordingly, Aleppo and Antioch flourished and served Byzantium as a base for supplies: yet they were Saracenic; and, in an evil hour, the Government of Romanus II determined to destroy them. In 962 the future Emperor, Nicephorus Phocas, began a series of frightful campaigns. He utterly devastated the lovely valley of the Orontes, closing Syria to commerce, and forcing trade to pass through the Red Sea and the mouths of the Nile. Thenceforward, cargoes changed hands at Cairo, not at Bassora; and the burden of the chronic war against the Greeks was shifted from the Caliphs of Bagdad to the Sultans of Egypt.

This stride westward made Cairo and Venice. Cairo became the seat of the wholesale trade; while the position of Constantinople grew geographically eccentric. Moreover, Venice prevailed as a market. Egypt, though rich in luxuries, lacked material of war, which was abundant in Europe. Constantinople rejected such trade with her enemy: but the Venetians sold greedily; and, therefore, Oriental traffic ascended the Adriatic, while Byzantium shared the fate of Bassora and Bagdad. The Venetian marine grew with her commerce. By the middle of the eleventh century it commanded the Mediterranean; and, with the Crusades, northern Italy received an impulsion which raised it to undisputed economic supremacy. In 1204 the Doge, Henry Dandolo, stormed the works of the Golden Horn, and carried home the accumulated treasure of five hundred years.

Movement is the law of nature. Venice fell through the energy of the very maritime genius she had fostered. In 1497 Vasco da Gama discovered a cheaper route to India than by the Levant. The arrival of his fleet at Calcutta was the signal for exchanges to pass at a leap from the Adriatic to the North Sea; prostrating Venice, Genoa, Pisa, and Florence, raising Antwerp and Amsterdam, and heaving up the great convulsions of the sixteenth century.

The last journey of exchanges westward began when Clive disturbed the existing social status by pouring into England the plunder of Bengal. Plassey was fought in 1757. In the process of readjustment, Napoleon attempted to strangle England, as Chosroes had tried to strangle Byzantium. He failed; but the equilibrium then attained after forty years of war, now seems tottering to its fall.

Year by year since 1870, when France discovered symptoms of advanced decay, the gangrene has eaten deeper. Last year Greece passed into the throes of dissolution; this year Italy and Austria are in hardly suppressed revolution; while Spain is being dismembered, and in her disintegration has involved the United States in war. The United States thus stands face to face with the gravest conjecture that can confront a

people. She must protect the outlets of her trade, or
run the risk of suffocation. Those outlets are maritime,
and are threatened by the same coalition which threatens England. The policy of Continental Europe is
not new. It is the policy of Napoleon and of Chosroes;
for Russia seeks to substitute land for water communication. In a few years Peking, and probably the Yangtse, will be connected with Moscow and Berlin by
rail; and then entirely new conditions will prevail. At
present, Continental interests in China are trifling.
The following table, from a French source (*L'Illustration* of January 23, 1897) may be trusted not to belittle
them:

External Commerce of China for 1894

Total, Francs 1,216,000,000, distributed thus:

Country	Millions of Francs	Country	Millions of Francs
England	857	Japan	77
United States	108	Russia	51
Western Europe	104	Others	19

This estimate placed the interest of the United
States in 1894 at one-eighth of that of England, and
at about one-eleventh of the whole; Russia's part
amounted to only one twenty-fourth; and France,
Germany, and Belgium, combined, represented one-
twelfth. In a valuable report just issued by Mr.

O'Beirne, of the British Diplomatic Service, the trade of the United States with China is reckoned at "one-seventh of the entire trade of the Empire in 1896," as "more than 50 per cent larger than the German exports," and as having increased "126 per cent in ten years." England and the United States have, therefore, today a stake in the Far East more than six times greater than that of Russia, Germany, France, and Belgium, combined.

Nor is the present the matter of chief concern. The expansion of any country must depend on the market for its surplus product; and China is the only region which now promises almost boundless possibilities of absorption, especially in the way of iron for its railroads.

Like other Asiatics, the Russians are not maritime. No Oriental empire ever rested on a naval supremacy. Phoenicians and Arabs alike failed to hold their own upon the sea; and, therefore, the path of commerce has been deflected north toward Rome and London, instead of continuing due west by Carthage and Cadiz. A century ago Gibbon pointed out that Chosroes failed, as Artaxerxes had failed before him, because of the weakness of his marine—a weakness which contrasts with the vigor of the Greek, the Italian, the Dutch, and the English. The same flaw crippled Napoleon. Doubtless the difficulty of land transport contributed to his fall; but how far that difficulty has been removed by steam is undetermined. Possibly the change has been radical enough to permit an Asiatic race now to succeed, if backed by French capital, where the French themselves failed.

From the retail store to the empire, success in modern life lies in concentration. The active and economical organisms survive: the slow and costly perish. Just as the working of this law has produced, during the last century, unprecedented accumulations of capital controlled by single minds, so it has produced political agglomerations such as Germany, the British Empire, and the United States. The probability is that hereafter the same causes will generate still larger coalitions directed toward certain military and economic ends. One strong stimulant thereto is the cost of armaments. For example, England and the United States combined could easily maintain a fleet which would make them supreme at sea; while as rivals they might be ruined. The acceleration of movement, which is thus concentrating the strong, is so rapidly crushing the weak that the moment seems at hand when two great competing systems will be left pitted against each other, and the struggle for survival will begin. Already America has been drawn into war over the dismemberment of one dying civilization; and it cannot escape the conflict which must be waged over the carcass of another. Even now the hostile forces are converging on the shores of the Yellow Sea; the English and the Germans to the south; Russia at Port Arthur, covering Peking; while Japan hungers for Korea, the key to the great inlet. The Philippine Islands, rich, coal-bearing, and with fine harbors, seem a predestined base for the United States in a conflict which probably is as inevitable as that with Spain. It is in vain that men talk of keeping free from entanglements. Nature is omnipotent; and nations must float with the tide. Whither the exchanges flow, they must follow; and they will follow as long as their vitality endures. How and when the decisive moment may come is beyond conjecture. It may be tomorrow, or it may not be for years. If Russia and Germany can shape events, it will not be until their navies and railroads are complete. But these great catastrophes escape human control. The collapse of France might convulse society in an instant. Whether agreeable to them or not, economic exigencies seem likely to constrain Englishmen and Americans to combine for their own safety, and possibly hesitation about their policy may be as dangerous as indecision in war.

Friends and enemies now agree that an Anglo-Saxon alliance, directed to attain certain common ends, might substantially make its own terms; but how it would stand, if opposed by a power capable of massing troops at pleasure in the heart of China, is less clear. What is tolerably certain, however, is that, with the interior distributing points well garrisoned, discrimination might go very far toward turning the commercial current against the maritime races. Suppose such discrimination were to succeed, and China were to be closed, the center of exchanges might move east from the Thames; and then London and New York could hardly fail to fall into geographical eccentricity. Before the discoveries of Vasco da Gama, Venice and Florence were relatively more energetic and richer than they. On the other hand, if an inference may be drawn from the past, Anglo-Saxons have little to fear in a trial of strength; for they have been the most successful of adventurers. They have risen to fortune by days, like Plassey, the Heights of Abraham, and Manila; and although no one can be certain, before it has again been tested, that the race has preserved its ancient martial quality, at least aggression seems a less dangerous alternative than quiescence. The civilization which does not advance declines: the continent which, when Washington lived, gave a boundless field for the expansion of Americans, has been filled; and the risk of isolation promises to be more serious than the risk of an alliance. Such great movements, however, are not determined by argument, but are determined by forces which override the volition of man.

Should an Anglo-Saxon coalition be made, and succeed, it would alter profoundly the equilibrium of the world. Exchanges would then move strongly westward; and existing ideas would soon be as obsolete as those of a remote antiquity. Probably human society would then be absolutely dominated by a vast combination of peoples whose right wing would rest upon the British Isles, whose left would overhang the middle provinces of China, whose center would approach the Pacific, and who would encompass the Indian Ocean as though it were a lake, much as the Romans encompassed the Mediterranean.

The New Struggle for Life
Among Nations

THE phase of civilization through which mankind is now passing opened in 1870. For many years previous to the German victory a regular quickening of competition, caused by a steady acceleration of movement, had been undermining the equilibrium reached at Waterloo; but the new era only began after the collapse of France. Within the generation which has followed that catastrophe, the same forces, acting with gathering energy, have profoundly altered the conditions of life, and promise portentous changes in the future. Everywhere society tends to become organized in greater and denser masses, the more vigorous and economical mass destroying the less active and the more wasteful. Thus, Latin Europe has rotted from end to end of the Continent, China is disintegrating, and England seems destined to lose her pre-eminence as the heart of the world's industry and finance. On the other hand, Germany has grown to be the center of an entirely new economic system, Russia is rapidly absorbing all northern Asia as far as the Yang-tse River, and the United States has been converted from the most pacific of nations into an armed and aggressive community.

Where these changes will lead is beyond prediction, but their advance may be followed from year to year, and, judging by the past, some estimate may be formed of the difficulties which confront America, and of the power of the combination of adversaries who may possibly assail her.

Up to 1873, England as a manufacturer stood without a rival, and she sold her wares at such a profit that, after exhausting domestic investments, a large surplus remained which she placed abroad, chiefly in Argentina, Australia, India, and America. The money so placed served in no small degree as the basis for the development of these countries. The first and most striking effect of the sharpened competition which followed 1870 was the advent of a period of falling prices, which soon began to work extensive complications. Agriculture suffered first, and in Great Britain, by 1879, farming had ceased to pay. Thenceforward the islands produced less and less food, the population buying their provisions abroad. Thus it happened that at the moment when the profit on exports withered under competition, a drain set in to pay for bread and meat, which increased with the growth of the nation.

Apparently the balance of trade, which England still held on other commodities, and the income from foreign investments, proved insufficient to meet this drain; for, to pay their debts, the British proceeded to realize on their loans, and the liquidation which followed precipitated a crisis probably without a parallel. Its course seems to have been somewhat as follows:

Until 1876, the United Kingdom easily imported all the gold she needed both to maintain an expanding currency and to supply her parts; but in 1877 the tide turned, and the next decade showed a net export of upward of $11,000,000, to say nothing of what was absorbed in the parts. This loss represented coin directly withdrawn from circulation. A severe contraction followed, prices fell nearly 40 per cent, and by 1886 distress had grown so sharp that, to obtain relief, sales were made of foreign securities. As these progressed, gold imports began again; in 1890 they even reached $45,000,000; but the strain of payment ruined the debtors. In 1890 Argentina collapsed, and carried down the Barings; in 1891 Australia followed; while in 1893 the United States was shaken to its center. Last of all has come the turn of India. There, within three years, society has seemed at moments on the brink of dissolution.

To speculate upon the final consequences of this financial revolution would be futile; but one of its immediate effects seems to be the displacement of the economic center of the world, thus engendering an unstable equilibrium which threatens war. All the energetic races have been plunged into a contest for the possession of the only markets left open capable of absorbing surplus manufactures, since all are forced to encourage exports to maintain themselves. A good illustration is the case of the United States. The pressure of creditors has acted like a bounty on exports.

From 1848 to 1876, with the exception of three years—1858, 1862, and 1874—the imports of the United States exceeded the exports. The total excess of exports of those three years amounted only to about $29,000,000, while the excess of imports of the single year 1869 reached $131,000,000. In 1876 England began contraction, and instantaneously the figures were reversed. Of the last twenty-two years, but three—1888, 1889, and 1893—have shown an excess of imports, which altogether came, in round numbers, to $50,000,000, while the excess of exports mounted forthwith to prodigious figures: in 1877 to $151,000,000, in 1878, to $257,000,000, in 1879, to $264,000,000, and for the first eleven months of 1898, without reckoning silver, the balance touched the huge sum of $538,000,000, or, taken altogether, nearly $2,000,000 for every working day of the year.

A change so vast and so sudden is, perhaps, without

precedent. Meanwhile the needs of Great Britain appear to increase. Last year her trade deficit reached £157,000,000 (a sum larger than anyone has ever computed as the return of her foreign investments and the earnings of her shipping), and the first ten months of this year (1898) exceed the corresponding months of last by upward of £17,000,000. (The adverse balance for 1897 was £176,594,207.) For the first time, the sale of our securities has not sufficed to balance the account, and the recent large inflow of gold may possibly foreshadow the exhaustion of the American floating debt abroad.

Be this as it may, no one can fail to perceive how the pressure of creditors has stimulated the export of manufactures from the United States. About the year 1887 our people were peremptorily called upon to pay their debts at a faster rate than their yearly earnings permitted. The decrease in the value of agricultural products made it impossible for these to be sold in sufficient quantities to fill the gap; enough gold to cover the deficit was not to be had; nothing remained but insolvency or the forcing down of the price of manufactures until we could undersell our creditors on their own ground. Impossible as such a feat once seemed, this has been done. Our iron and steel, in particular, are now the cheapest in the world, and, accordingly, are received even in London in payment of balances. India has been subjected to the same suction, and the growth of the Indian exports is almost as remarkable as the growth of the exports of the United States.

How long English accumulations will last is immaterial, since, in one form or another, they will doubtless suffice for the immediate future. The upshot of the whole matter, therefore, is that America has been irresistibly impelled to produce a large industrial surplus—a surplus, should no change occur, which will be larger in a few years than anything ever before known. Upon the existence of this surplus hinges the future, for the United States must provide sure and adequate outlets for her products, or be in danger of gluts more dangerous to her society than many panics such as 1873 and 1893.

Although falling prices may discourage new enterprises, they certainly stimulate production in factories already established, until they have to be closed by actual loss. A cotton mill, for example, which clears but a mill a yard must, roughly speaking, sell, to earn its dividend, double the number of yards that would be necessary were its profit two mills. Accordingly, large sales and small returns are accepted as an axiom of modern trade. A fall in prices, therefore, stimulates production, and production reacts on prices; the tendency being to dislocate the whole social system of any people where a surplus exists, unless a vent can be found abroad to sustain the market. The decline of the West India Islands offers a striking example of the operation of this process.

Even before the Franco-German War, Prussia tried to foster the export of beet sugar by drawbacks which amounted to a bounty; but the effect on commerce only became marked after the consolidation of the Empire, and serious about the year 1881. Between 1881 and 1896, however, unrefined cane sugar fell, in London, from 21.09 shillings to 10.85 shillings the hundredweight, and refined suffered in proportion. The supply, on the other hand, swelled enormously. The total production of raw sugar was 3,799,000 tons in 1882, and 7,278,000 tons at the outbreak of the Cuban insurrection in 1894. The chief outlet for the cane sugar of the British West Indies had always been England, and when the Germans flooded the English market, so grave a glut ensued that Lord Salisbury's Government sent a commission to the islands to examine their condition. It is hardly an exaggeration to say that the report which followed is among the most interesting public documents of modern times.

The commissioners found that, as the price of sugar sank, the production grew until the outbreak in Cuba, when the cane fell off a million tons; yet this shrinkage of the cane only encouraged fresh exports of beet, and values continued to diminish until, in 1896, Germany doubled her bounties. The effect of this policy upon the West Indies was disastrous. From prosperity the islands sank into misery.

The report states that, in view of all the circumstances attending the production of sugar,

the West Indies is threatened with such a reduction [of the industry] in the immediate future as may not in some of the colonies differ very greatly from extinction, and must seriously affect them all [with the exception of such as no longer plant the cane]. The consequences are likely to be of a very serious character. The immediate result would be a great want of employment for the labouring classes, and the rates of wages, which have already fallen, would in all probability be still further reduced. The public revenue would fall off, and the Governments of some of Your Majesty's possessions would be unable to meet the absolutely necessary public expenditure, including interest on debt.[1]

The Chairman, Sir Henry Norman, went much further. The inhabitants of British Guiana and of the Barbados would

be without the means of purchasing imported articles of food, or of paying taxes . . . The planters must be ruined

[1] Report of the West India Royal Commission, p. 7.

. . . the tradesmen, artisans, and labouring classes will suffer privation, and probably become discontented and restless, and the revenue will be so crippled as to render it impossible to carry on the Government, even on the most economical scale, in any condition at all approaching to efficiency.[2]

Even in the case of Jamaica, with other industries to fall back on, "there will be much distress, and [her] resources . . . will be severely taxed." When a man like General Norman could write thus of some of the best-administered communities in the world, the condition of Cuba may be imagined.

In Cuba the crisis became acute in 1894, when sugar fell in London from fourteen to twelve shillings the hundredweight, followed the next year by a fall of two shillings more. The old system of planting collapsed, the relations of capital and labor were dislocated, the exactions of Spain made the life of the agriculturists impossible, and the revolt, which had long been expected, began. The revolt involved the United States with Spain, and thus the inroads of Germany on the London sugar market precipitated the recent war.

If, however, the stoppage of the outlet of the export trade of so petty a portion of the earth's surface as the West Indies produced the catastrophes of the last four years, the future course of the United States, with its

[2] Ibid., p. 73.

vast and growing surplus, becomes the most momentous question of the age. No theory has ever proved more fallacious than the dogma that the cheapest goods command the world's market. The whole protective system of modern times demonstrates the contrary, for this system is principally designed to control international commerce. No country has gone further in this direction than America, and, doubtless, exclusion has proved effective as long as home consumption has exceeded home production. From the moment, however, that production exceeds consumption all conditions are changed. Then the surplus must seek a vent abroad, and there are clear indications that a great coalition is coming into being whose aim is to exclude the United States from those countries which should be her natural outlet.

From the dawn of time, commerce has flowed from east to west in the track of the migrations of the races. The last of these great migrations began at the close of the Middle Ages, when Europeans succeeded in crossing the ocean which had heretofore stopped them. Of the four chief nations bordering the Atlantic, the Spanish, French, Dutch, and English, the advantage at first lay with the Spanish. Spain, however, lacked energy; her fate was sealed in the maritime wars which culminated with the Armada, since which time she has served as a prey to her rivals. The French proved more

determined. For three generations they fought stub-
bornly, though fruitlessly. They lost Canada on the
Heights of Abraham, their navy at the Nile and Trafalgar, and from 1805 transit by sea to them was closed.
In that age water offered the only ready path toward expansion; but the French persevered even when
driven from the ocean. Turning suddenly to the eastward, they marched toward Asia. They reached
Moscow. There they halted, and from that day their
decline began. They were forced slowly back within
their own borders, and since Waterloo the Anglo-
Saxons have taken what pleased them of the vacant
portions of the world.

For nearly half a century, Continental Europe, shut
in between the sea and the impassable wastes of Asia,
lay stifling, until at length the railroad made communication by land relatively practicable. Then prodigious
changes set in. As the railroad system approached ma-
turity Paris ceased to be the chief seat of Continental
energy, and the convulsion of 1870 marked the passage
of the Rhine by the focus of industry and finance. The
war indemnity exacted by Germany of France trans-
ported beyond the Rhine, almost in a mass, 1000 millions of dollars (5000 millions of francs). This alone
was almost enough to establish in Germany a financial
preponderance, and other causes operated to the same
end. The march eastward cannot be mistaken. Perhaps

pig iron is as good as any gauge of industrial activity, and in the production of pig iron France has not held her own.

Between 1880 and 1896 the French output of pig iron advanced from 1,725,290 tons to 2,333,702, or at a rate slightly above 2 per cent a year. The German output, on the other hand, swelled from 2,729,038 tons to 6,360,982, an annual increment of 8⅓ per cent, while the Russian rose from 740,000 tons in 1889 to 1,747,000 in 1897, an average of 17 per cent.

A like phenomenon has appeared in transportation. In 1870 Cologne was doubtless the chief railway base for northern Europe east of the Rhine; now Breslau is its rival; and the railway system which then ended at Nizhni-Novgorod approaches Peking, and is projected as far as Hankow.

A displacement of energy has occurred proportionate to this movement. France alone is estimated to have lent Russia upwards of $400,000,000 for the Siberian railroad and other enterprises within the last ten years. All that Germany can spare of money, ability, and enterprise is swept into the current; and thus northern Europe and Asia, from the Bay of Biscay to the Yellow Sea, is solidifying into an economic mass whose heart lies at Berlin.

The capacity of this mass for absorbing adjacent populations is, seemingly, limitless. A few years ago

Manchuria was pure Chinese; now it is Russian; Peking is following Manchuria, and with Peking goes Shansi, with the richest coal and iron deposits of the world. Already the vast monster, stretching its tentacles far southward, is grasping Hankow, the Chicago of the Yangtse valley.

Whether it be upon the Rhine or the Amur, the policy of this Eastern civilization is the same. It is the old policy of Napoleon—the policy of exclusion. No better example could be found than the aggressions of Germany, who, since the consolidation of 1870, has deliberately ruined the West Indies by forcing her bounty-fed sugar on foreigners, while seeking by every device to exclude foreign products from her markets. Had the West Indies themselves, or Great Britain, their protector, been able to coerce Germany into abandoning her abnormal exports, the islands of the Gulf of Mexico would be as rich and happy as of yore. The same danger, on a vaster scale, threatens every exporting nation which allows its outlets to be closed, and a little consideration will suffice to show that, in the case of the United States, this danger is both real and near.

Speaking broadly, a century ago, the whole earth, outside of Europe and portions of Asia, lay open to colonization or conquest. In 1757 Clive won the battle of Plassey, and in 1760 the "industrial revolution" began in England. From 1760 to 1870 an expansion took place without a parallel in human experience, and after the defeat of France the Anglo-Saxons were substantially unopposed. This movement reached its limit between 1850 and 1870, with the opening up of California and Australia; but during the whole period all the originality and energy of mankind failed to meet the demand caused by the creation of the gigantic system of manufactures, of mining, and of credit, which then came into being. Consumption outran production, men seriously believed that a general glut was impossible, the margin of profit was broad, and waste counted for less, in the success or failure of enterprises, than activity and daring.

By 1870 the most tempting regions of the earth had been occupied, for the Anglo-Saxons had reached the Pacific. The rate of expansion accordingly began to decline, and as it declined, masses grew denser, competition sharpened, and prices fell. At length, as the century draws to a close, it is recognized, that the survival of individuals, corporations, and governments is determined by an economic struggle which tests their administrative efficiency more severely than private war ever tested courage. The last step of the advance was taken in the war with Spain. Then the Americans crossed the Pacific, and the two great branches of the Anglo-Saxon race met on the coast of China, having girdled the earth.

In the favored line, running from east to west, all the choicest territory has been occupied, besides most of what is accessible in the southern hemisphere. Eastern Asia now appears, without much doubt, to be the only district likely soon to be able to absorb any great increase of manufactures, and accordingly, Eastern Asia is the prize for which all the energetic nations are grasping. If the Continental coalition wins, that coveted region will be closed to its rivals.

Should it be so closed, the pressure caused by the stoppage of the current which has so long run westward might shake American society to its foundation, and would probably make the scale of life to which our people are habituated impossible.

From its infancy, civilization has advanced by two processes—the individual and the collective. In a very general way the Eastern races have tended toward collective systems, and the Western toward individual. The effect of these instincts is plainly visible in architecture. For example, there has never been a magnificent palace or tomb in England; while the remains of the royal dwellings of Assyria and Susiana are stupendous, the dwelling of a Byzantine emperor resembled a city in itself, and the Egyptian pyramids continue to be wonders of the world.

The Anglo-Saxon has been the most individual of races, and it reached high fortune under conditions which fostered individuality to a supreme degree. Such conditions prevailed when the world was vacant and steam began to make rapid movement possible; but all must perceive that, as masses solidify, the qualities of the pioneer will cease to be those that command success.

As expansion ceases, as competition quickens, and as prices fall, men consolidate in larger and denser masses, because, other things being equal, the administration of the largest mass is the cheapest. This tendency is already marked in every walk of life, particularly in those huge agglomerations called trusts. Hitherto the effect of the trust has not been to raise prices to the consumer, nor has it been to stimulate production. On the contrary, the trust has been organized to adjust the supply to the demand. Trusts must be profitable, therefore, because they economize wages and rent; and it is this economy of labor and elimination of waste which is the characteristic of modern civilization. But the concentration of which the result is an elimination of waste is nothing but a movement toward collectivism, and the relative rise of the peoples who excel in the collective methods has been accordingly contemporaneous with the advent of the great trusts in the West.

Perhaps the best example of the success of the collective method is the centralization of Germany and the organization of Russia. From its very birth, the Prussian Kingdom has been subjected to a pressure seldom equaled. Under this pressure the people consolidated in a singularly compact mass, developing a corporate administration powerful enough to succeed very generally in subordinating individual to general interests. It is to this quality that Prussia has owed her comparative gain on England.

All agree that the industrial success of Germany is largely due to the establishment of cheap and uniform rates of transportation, through state ownership of railways; while the industrial progress of Russia would have been impossible had not the Government been both railroad and mine owner, besides being banker and money-lender, and ready at any moment to promote industries, such as iron works, whenever individuals could not act advantageously.

England, on the other hand, has held her own neither as a manufacturer, as an exporter, nor as an agriculturist. Whereas in 1873 her exports amounted to £255,000,000, in 1897 they reached only £234,350,000. The loss on her agriculture has been estimated at $250,000,000 yearly. It is probably larger. The

British adverse trade balance is chiefly due to the importations of food which might be raised at home. That adverse balance has grown from £60,282,000 in 1873 to £157,055,000 in 1897.

If the English farmers are asked why their farms do not pay; why grazing, for which their pastures are peculiarly adapted, proves unprofitable, they have but one answer. They explain that high and unequal railroad rates make it possible to transport produce more cheaply from Chicago to London than from Somersetshire or Yorkshire to London. The same complaint is made by the iron trade. The inference is that, had England been able to act as energetically in her corporate capacity as Germany, had she subdued the opposition of individual interests and secured the German rates of transportation, her position as a competitor would be changed.

Applying the same measure to the United States, the same weak spot appears. The national characteristic is waste, and each year, as the margin of profit narrows, waste grows more dangerous. Under an exact administration one corporation will prosper, while its neighbor is ruined by slight leakage; and what holds true of the private enterprise holds equally true of those greatest of human ventures called governments.

Our national corporation was created to meet the wants of a scanty agricultural population at a time when movement was slow. It has now to deal with masses surpassing, probably, in bulk, any in the world. In consequence it operates slowly and imperfectly, or fails to operate at all. The Pennsylvania Railroad might as reasonably attempt to handle the traffic of 1898 with the staff of 1860 as the United States to deal with its affairs under Mr. McKinley with the appliances which barely sufficed for Jefferson or Jackson. We have just seen our army put on the field without a general staff, much after the method of 1812, and we have witnessed the consequences. We know what would have happened had we been opposed by a vigorous enemy. We wonder daily at our Treasury struggling with enormous banking transactions, without banking facilities; while our foreign service is so helpless, in its most important function of obtaining secret information, that the Government relied on daily papers for news of the Spanish fleet.

In short, in America there is no administration in the modern sense of the word. Every progressive nation is superior to us in organization, since every such nation has been reorganized since we began. That America has prospered under these conditions is due altogether to the liberal margin of profit obtainable in the United States, which has made extreme activity and individuality counterbalance waste. This margin of profit, due to expansion caused by the acquisition of

Louisiana and California, carried the country buoy-
antly until, under the pressure of English realization,
it was stimulated into producing an industrial surplus.
The time has now come when that surplus must be
sold abroad, or a glut must be risked like that which
has overtaken the West Indies. Today the nation has
to elect whether to continue to expand, cost what it
may, or to resign itself to the approach of a relatively
stationary period, when competition will force it to
abandon the individual for the collective mode of life.
Here the experience of the French is instructive. When
defeated in their attempts at expansion, they betook
themselves to economizing as few Western peoples
have ever done. They relieved competition in the wage
market by reducing the birthrate until the population
ceased to multiply; while in their families they habitually practiced a frugality unknown to Anglo-Saxons.
They succeeded in preserving their physical well-
being, but at the cost of their national vitality. As a
nation they have grown old, and are devoured by the
gangrene which attacks every stagnant society and
from which no patient recovers.

Parsimony is alien to our habits, and would hardly
become a national trait under pressure less severe than
that under which Germany slowly consolidated after
Jena, or under which France began to sink after Moscow. But if we are not prepared to reduce our scale of

life to the German or perhaps the Russian standard, if we are not prepared to accept the collective methods of administration with all that they imply, we must be prepared to fight our adversary, and we must arm in earnest.

Whether we like it or not, we are forced to compete for the seat of international exchanges, or, in other words, for the seat of empire. The prize is the most dazzling for which any people can contend, but it has usually been won only by the destruction of the chief competitor of the victor. Rome rose on the ruins of Carthage, and England on the collapse of Spain and France.

For upward of a thousand years the tendency of the economic center of the world has been to move westward, and the Spanish War has only been the shock caused by its passing the Atlantic. Probably, within two generations, the United States will have faced about, and its great interests will cover the Pacific, which it will hold like an inland sea. The natural focus of such a Pacific system would be Manila. Lying where all the paths of trade converge, from north and south, east and west, it is the military and commercial key to eastern Asia. Entrenched there, and backing on Europe, with force enough to prevent our competitors from closing the Chinese mainland against us by discrimination, there is no reason why the United States should not become a greater seat of wealth and power than ever was England, Rome, or Constantinople.

But to maintain such an empire presupposes an organization perfect in proportion to the weight it must support and the friction it must endure; and it is the perfecting of this organization, both military and civil, which must be the task of the next fifty years. For there is no possibility of self-deception. Our adversary is deadly and determined. Such are his jealousy of our power and his fear of our expansion, that to cripple us he would have gladly joined with Spain. But for the victory of Manila and the attitude of England, his fleets would last spring have been off our coasts. If we yield before him, he will stifle us.

If the coalition of France, Germany, and Russia succeeds in occupying and organizing the interior of China, if this coalition can control its trade and discriminate against our exports, it will have good prospects of throwing back a considerable surplus on our hands, for us to digest as best we can. In that event, America's possible destiny might be to approach the semistationary period of France, meanwhile entering into a competition with our rivals in regard to the cost of domestic life, of industrial production, and of public administration. In such a competition, success can only be won by surpassing the enemy in his own method, or in that concentration which reduces waste to a minimum. Such a concentration might, conceivably, be effected by the growth and amalgamation of great trusts until they absorbed the Government, or it might be brought about by the central corporation, called the Government, absorbing the trusts. In either event, the result would be approximately the same. The Eastern and Western continents would be competing for the most perfect system of State Socialism.

England's Decadence in the West Indies

THAT within ten years the world has entered upon a new stage of development seems self-evident; and it appears equally self-evident that the spot where the old system has broken down lies in the West Indies. But when another step is taken, and the causes are sought, which have led to the decay of the archipelago of the Caribbean, we enter upon some of the most absorbing problems of modern civilization.

Before attempting to examine details, it may be simpler to look for a moment at first principles. We may assume, as an axiom, that men, like other animals, must be capable of obtaining their subsistence under the conditions to which they are born; for, if incapable, they must starve. We must also assume that the individual, to prosper, must have the flexibility to adapt himself to the changes going on about him; for, should he be rigid, he would be superseded by someone more pliable. Hence, human customs, laws, and empires probably owe their rise and fall to the exigencies of that competition for food, which, from the beginning, has sifted those destined to survive from those doomed to perish. Consequently, society can never reach a permanent equilibrium: nothing can be constant but change.

The deduction from these premises is, that the decline of the West Indies must be due to an inability on the part of the population to keep pace with competition. The causes of this failure may be complex: but in the end, the failure itself must represent a relative loss of energy; and it is with this loss of energy that we now have to deal.

If it be true that the English who, as well as the Spanish, inhabit the Western tropics, are ceasing to be able to hold their own with other races, in the struggle for life, the effects cannot fail to be manifold. At the outset, for example, one of two results must apparently follow: either this whole region must be absorbed in some more elastic economic system, or it must sink to the level of Haiti. At present the drift is toward the United States. But for the United States to assimilate and administer this mass successfully implies a simplification and centralization of her own administrative system; and no forecast about whither a further consolidation of the Republic would lead is now possible.

Nevertheless, that such a consolidation is now actually going on about us is highly probable; wherefore, the study of the sequence of events which has determined the ruin of some of the fairest gardens of the earth should interest Americans, since their own destiny may be inexorably linked with that of a dependency which they may be constrained to absorb.

Down to the battle of Waterloo, perhaps no landed property had ever proved more profitable than the sugar estates of the Caribbean; and before the advent of the East Indian nabob the West Indian planter filled, in the popular fancy, the figure of the ideal millionaire. Judged by modern standards, his profits might indeed be called fabulous. Tooke's tables of prices begin with 1782; but, as the years from 1783 to 1789 were peaceful, the interval probably represents fairly enough the ordinary trade of the last century. Between 1783 and 1789 Muscovado sugar ranged somewhere about £35 the ton; during the next ten years the war forced it to about £60; and as late as 1815 it brought £63. These values are tolerably reliable; but it is harder to fix the cost of production . In those lavish days management was loose, and nobody knew precisely what he spent; but, judging by the expense involved in the old processes, which are yet used on many of the islands, there seems no reason to suppose that Muscovado cost the competent planter, as a rule, much more than £20 a ton to produce. On the other hand, he may have worked more cheaply, since he used slave labor. At this time, also, and down to about 1850, colonial sugar paid less than half the duty levied on foreign products under the British tariff, and therefore held a practical monopoly of the home market.

Reckoning rum and molasses as part of the sugar crop, a good estate, well handled, might yield nearly the equivalent of three tons to the acre; therefore, the net profit in ordinary seasons approximated £45 the acre, and during war, £120. In other words, one of the small Barbados plantations of two hundred acres of cane represented an income of $45,000 as an average, and $120,00 as a maximum.

Modern expansion began with the English industrial revolution, dating from about 1760. To both the east and the west the world lay open; and competition could gain small purchase on prices in a society growing so vigorously that it could absorb far more than it could produce. That era reached its climax with Waterloo; and during that era the West Indies enjoyed their highest fortune. As Dr. Morris has rather sadly observed in his recent report to the British Government: [1]

Jamaica had nearly attained the meridian of its prosperity in 1787, just one hundred and ten years ago. It

[1] Report of the West India Royal Commission, Appendix A, p. 139.

would be useful to contrast the quantity and value of its exports [then] with the exports of today:

Product	1787	1896
Sugar	42,028 tons	22,995 tons
Rum	2,543,025 gallons	1,881,100 gallons
Molasses	6,416 gallons	. . . . . .
[Other items are omitted]		
Total value	£2,283,728	£1,775,016

In 1805, nevertheless, when the war had raised prices 50 per cent, Jamaican trade dwarfed even this showing. In that year she actually sold 150,352 hogsheads of sugar, and more than 5,000,000 gallons of rum; the price of a ton of Muscovado sugar being £53, while 4s. 9d. was paid for a gallon of rum. In 1897 raw sugar brought £9 13s. the ton, and rum 1s. 4d. the gallon. Indeed, from 1790 onward for a quarter of a century, the gains of England on all sides were prodigious; for she kept Continental Europe under blockade, and exacted what prices she pleased for imports. Many tropical products, for example, such as spices and sugar, which had become almost necessaries, could only reach France by water; and, as England held the sea, she imposed her own terms on all the territory occupied by the French. During those years the tide of commercial exchanges reached its flood in favor of the United Kingdom; and then she amassed much of those unprecedented accumulations on whose income she has of late relied to balance the growing trade deficit caused by her purchases of foreign food. Yet, even in the moment of victory, and, perhaps, because of the completeness of her triumph, Great Britain laid the seeds of a competition which has since gnawed her vitals—a competition which has, moreover, ruined the West Indies, formerly the flower of her empire.

Since the dawn of history two forms of centralization, evolved through different processes of transportation, have contended for supremacy. The one, which may be called the Continental system, based upon the highway, found its amplest expression in Rome; the other, which may be described as the maritime, is the offspring of the sea, and has served as the vehicle for the consolidation of that economic organism which has permeated the modern world, and whose heart has been London. Before the discovery of the compass and the quadrant made the ocean navigable, the Continental system usually predominated. From the Crusades to the collapse of France in 1870, the maritime had the advantage. Recently, the railroad, by bringing the cost of land and water carriage nearer an equality, has tended to inflame the conflict, without, as yet, deciding the victory.

The Continental system became incarnate in Napoleon. Generations in advance of his age, with the eye of genius, he saw that between movement by land and movement by water there existed a rivalry which could know no other arbiter than battle; and he fought to the end. Feeling the coil of the blockade slowly strangling him, he strove to make his country self-sufficing, while striking at the vitals of his enemy. Rightly regarding the distant dependencies as the members which fed the heart at London, he contemplated a march upon India by land, at the same time that he attacked the sugar islands by a policy more insidious and deadly than open war.

From an early period Bonaparte speculated on the possibility of making sugar from the beet; and in 1808 he wrote to scientific men pressing them to investigate the subject. In 1811 he had become certain of success; and early in that year he outlined, for his Minister of the Interior, a policy of state encouragement of the domestic sugar industry which, in substance, has been adopted by the chief Continental nations, and which survives to this day. In one paragraph the Emperor declared, "that, by thus employing a small acreage, France might succeed in escaping the tribute she paid to foreigners."

Yet even Bonaparte failed to grasp the full bearings of the system of retaliation which he invented, and which was destined, before the century closed, to play a chief part in the recentralization of the world. He fell almost immediately; and the progress of competition is slow. In 1828 the French sugar production reached only 2,685 tons; in 1836, 49,000; in 1847, 64,000; nor was it until after 1855, when the Continent had begun to feel the acceleration of movement caused by the railroad, and the English had opened their markets to the bounty-fed product by establishing uniform duties in foreign and colonial sugar, that the manufacture attained 100,000 tons. Then, however, the advance became rapid; and in 1862 England imported 40,000 tons of her rival's produce, against 193,000 drawn from the colonies of the Caribbean Sea. In 1871, when Germany took the place theretofore held by France, the plantations already lagged behind: in that year England imported 232,000 tons of Continental beet, as against 213,000 of West Indian cane.

This gradual occupation of the French market, and this invasion of the English, caused a regular fall in the price of sugar and its derivatives, in spite of the gold discoveries of 1849, which raised all other values. In discussing the interval between 1850 and 1862, Jevons [2] has remarked:

"Sugar and spirits stand out as the only two obstinate and real exceptions to a general rise of prices; but

[2] *Investigations in Currency and Finance*, p. 55.

again, as Jamaica rum, quoted for spirits, is made from sugar, they might be said to form only a single exception."

Although in 1870 the vigor of France had long been on the ebb, the French attack proved serious. In 1858 Muscovado sold for 27s. 10d. the hundredweight; in 1867, when German consolidation began, it had dropped to 22s. 4d.; and in 1868 the long Cuban convulsion opened which has lasted till today.

The migration eastward of the center of the Continental system, whose focus, under Napoleon, had been at Paris, occasioned the rise of Germany. But though the capital city might change, the instinct of the centralized mass remained constant; and the Emperor of Germany, in assuming the position of the Emperor of France, assumed his methods and his attitude toward England. The chief difference between the two civilizations lay in a difference of energy.

The figures which tell of the impact of this new power upon its maritime rival may well be called dramatic. Within less than a generation from the coronation at Versailles of the German successor of Napoleon, English sugar had been substantially driven from the English market, the West Indies had been ruined, Cuba had been ravaged with fire and sword, Spain had been crushed by the United States, the United States had been thrown upon the coast of Asia, and the world had been sent plunging forward toward a new equilibrium. Meanwhile, sugar had been forced down to £9 a ton.

In 1873 the total export of beet sugar from France and Germany stood thus: France, 221,000 tons; Germany, 24,000 tons. In 1896 the imports into England alone stood thus: from France, 143,000 tons; from Germany, 755,000 tons. In 1871 England imported 455,962 tons of cane and 232,850 of beet; in 1896, 382,000 tons of cane and 1,144,000 of beet.

Witnesses testified before a commission in London that, during recent years, the refining trade had undergone a "progressive process of extinction," and that whereas it then produced wealth to the extent of £2,000,000 a year, it would, if healthy, yield £6,000,000.[3]

Taken in all its ramifications, this destruction of the sugar interest may probably be reckoned the heaviest financial blow that a competitor has ever dealt Great Britain, unless the injury to her domestic agriculture by the fall in the price of wheat be esteemed a loss through competition. Roughly, it may be computed somewhat as follows:

[3] Report of West India Royal Commission, Appendix C, 1, Part 1, pp. 153-4.

Assuming that, toward 1880, the British West Indies exported, in round numbers, 300,000 tons of sugar, 10,000,000 gallons of molasses, and 5,000,000 gallons of rum, and calculating the profit on the basis of 1789, we reach a total of about £5,000,000 for sugar, and of, perhaps, £1,500,000 more for molasses and rum. This £6,500,000 has been obliterated. To this must be added the shrinkage of purchasing power for new machinery, clothes, and food, which are reckoned under the head of "Cost of Production," the diminution of freights, the decay of the home-refining trade, and the blight of the whole archipelago, more especially the complete arrest of the growth of wonderful islands like Dominica and St. Lucia, now almost wildernesses, and of the vast province of Guiana, capable of being turned into one of the most fruitful portions of the earth—"At once the largest and most valuable of the British West Indian colonies, [whose] capabilities of development are practically unlimited." [4] What such a check has meant to Great Britain is beyond human computation. In the words of a pamphlet of the last century:

Our sugar colonies are of the utmost consequence and importance to Great Britain. They have been equal to the mines of the Spanish West Indies, and have contributed in

[4] Report of Dr. Morris, Appendix A, p. 83.

a particular manner to the trade, navigation, and wealth of this kingdom.[5]

Without dispute, whatever might have been done, sugar must have fallen in value; but these questions are always questions of degree. Had the mother country protected the interests of her colonies so far as to keep them on an equal footing with their competitors, that is to say, had she counteracted by her tariff the advantage given by Germany to her exporters by subsidies, the decline in price might not have exceeded economies made possible by improved machinery and concentration of property. According to the witnesses before the West India Royal Commission, the cost of manufacturing a ton of sugar has been reduced, within twenty years, from about £18 to £8 or £10 a ton.

Germany has not ruined the West Indies by legitimate competition, but by an adherence to Napoleon's policy of attack, which was a military measure. For nearly three generations the chief Continental nations have, with hostile intent, artificially stimulated the export of sugar, and have increased the stimulant as prices have fallen, in order to counteract the loss to the manufacturer. In August 1896, Germany and Austria doubled their bounties: in the following spring France advanced hers. Admitting, therefore, the success of

[5] *The Importance of the Sugar Colonies to Great Britain*, 1731, pp. 35-6.

Napoleon's war policy, one of the most interesting problems of our time is the cause which has rendered England vulnerable to this onslaught; for the course of civilization promises to hinge on the ability of Great Britain to maintain the economic ascendency she won at Trafalgar and Waterloo.

If space permitted, nothing would be easier than to demonstrate that, although in 1815 London was the heart of the maritime system, the United Kingdom did not achieve an undisputed economic supremacy until about 1835. Moreover, the supremacy was short, lasting only a generation, and ending with the rise of Germany in 1870. There is no mistaking this period; for it bears in its thought, its literature, its art, and its public policy, the impress of the force which created it. It was the age of the Manchester School, of Cobden, of Bright, and of Mill. But Cobden, Bright, and Manchester doctrines were phenomena which attended the advent of a new ruling class. A social revolution, which had been in progress for nearly a century, was consummated between 1840 and 1850; England passed from a rural into an urban community; and immediately a new era opened. The opening of this era is marked with equal clearness upon the pages of the Census and of the Statute Book. In 1841 the urban population of England and Wales numbered 7,679,737 souls; the rural, 8,229,395. In 1851 the urban population had increased to 9,213,942; the rural, only to 8,713,667. In 1846 Peel's administration repealed the Corn Laws: in 1848 Lord John Russell's administration equalized the sugar duties by putting colonial and foreign sugar on the same footing.

The power of the ancient rural population fell in 1846, with the repeal of the Corn Laws; and this event marked the rise of a new social stratum to control, who thenceforward used the machinery of government, as rulers always use it, for their own advantage. Inertia is, however, the bane of every aristocracy, be it an aristocracy of the rich or of the poor. By nature, man is lazy, working only under compulsion; and when he is strong he will always live, as far as he can, upon the labor or the property of the weak. The Romans fed themselves by taxing the provinces after their conquest, and degenerated; the Spaniards decayed when they could empty the mines of Mexico and Peru at no further sacrifice of energy than exterminating the natives; and slaveholders are notoriously indolent. So it has been, in a greater or lesser degree, with the British industrial class. The industrial population consists of two sections, the wage earners and the capitalists—sections hostile to each other, but apt to be united against those whom they can coerce. Certainly, they have always been at one in demanding cheap food—the capitalists, so that wages might not rise; the hands, that they might live at ease. To attain their end they have consistently sacrificed the farmers, as the Romans sacrificed the provincials; and the West Indian planters have but shared in the general agricultural ruin.

The human mind is so constituted that whatever benefits an individual seems to that individual to bene-fit the race; consequently, institutions like slavery and polygamy, and trades like usury, piracy, and slaving, have never lacked defenders on moral grounds. Anal-ogously, the English have justified the practical con-fiscation of the sugar estates, on the ground that, though the planters might be ruined, the nation at large enjoyed cheap sugar, thereby reaping a prepon-derating economic advantage. Nevertheless, eliminat-ing abstract justice, as never having decided public policy, it is not clear that the English, as a community, have reaped any economic advantage from cheap sugar; while, on the other hand, they have certainly lost by the destruction of the colonies. A few figures will make this proposition plain.

In 1869, before the collapse of France, and when the sugar islands were still relatively prosperous, Eng-lishmen consumed, on the average, 42 pounds of sugar per capita, annually. That this is enough for either health or reasonable enjoyment is proved by the fact that few peoples use so much today. For example, in 1896 Italy consumed 7.19 lbs. per capita; Spain, 12.67 lbs.; Germany, 27.14 lbs.; and France, 28.24 lbs.

In the United States, where the use of sweets is said to be injuriously excessive, only 35 lbs. per capita was consumed in 1869, and 60.3 lbs. in 1898. In England during 1895-7 every human being, including babies, invalids, and paupers, disposed, on the average, of nearly 4 oz. of sugar a day, or 84.77 lbs. a year. In other words, each citizen spent for sugar in those years almost exactly what he spent in 1869, the difference being that he doubled an already ample allowance.

Furthermore, neither from the economic nor the sanitary standpoint do the uses to which this extra sugar ration is put seem satisfactory. One of the chief of these appears to be to encourage drinking. Though the exports of beer from England show a tendency to decline, brewing grows apace. Twenty-seven gallons a year per capita, counting women and children, is surely enough. In America, though the amount of spirits drunk is the same, 15½ gallons of beer suffice; and American beer is light. Twenty-seven and one-quarter gallons was the measure for England in 1883; yet in 1897 it had swelled to 31½ gallons, an expansion at the rate of about 1 per cent a year. But, fast as brewing grows, the weight of sugar used in the beer grows faster. In 1883 the public put up with something less than 4¾ lbs. of sugar to the barrel: in 1897 it demanded between 8 and 9 lbs.

The same tendency toward extravagance appears throughout the list of imported articles of food. The ordinary citizen buys 63 per cent more foreign bacon and ham, 58 per cent more butter, 162 per cent more beef, and 1 lb. more tea annually than he did fourteen years ago. Yet, in 1883, Britons had not the reputation of being underfed.

This spread of self-indulgence would be without significance were it accompanied by a corresponding accretion of energy; but the industrial class of England has never learned that a larger cost of living must find its compensation in additional economy in production. On the one hand, trade unions have enforced shorter hours and withstood labor-saving machines; on the other, capitalists have failed to consolidate entire trades under a single management, and thereby reduce salaries and rent to a minimum.

Perhaps no better gauge can exist of the energy of a great industrial and exporting nation—especially a nation like England, which has practically attained its full internal development—than the amount of its per capita exports taken through a series of years. The subjoined table shows that, while Germany has remained stationary, and America has bounded forward, England, during the last generation, has retrograded.

TABLE SHOWING PROPORTION PER CAPITA OF THE EXPORTS OF MERCHANDISE OF THE UNITED KINGDOM, THE UNITED STATES, AND GERMANY DURING THE PERİOD 1869–97

Year	United Kingdom			United States	Germany		
	£	s.	d.	Dollars	£	s.	d.
1869	6	2	7	7.29			
1870	6	7	11	9.77			
1871	7	1	7	10.83			
1872	8	1	0	10.55	Data for these 8 years are incomplete		
1873	7	18	10	12.12			
1874	7	7	9	13.31			
1875	6	16	6	11.36			
1876	6	1	3	11.64			
1877	5	18	11	12.72	3	4	10
1878	5	14	1	14.30	3	7	9
1879	5	12	2	14.29	3	4	11
1880	6	9	5	16.43	3	4	10
1881	6	14	0	17.23	3	5	9
1882	6	16	10	13.97	3	10	0
1883	6	14	8	14.98	3	12	3
1884	6	10	6	13.20	3	10	0
1885	5	18	4	12.94	3	1	5
1886	5	17	2	11.60	3	3	8
1887	6	1	3	11.98	3	6	8
1888	6	7	2	11.40	3	8	5
1889	6	13	11	11.92	3	3	3
1890	7	0	7	13.50	3	7	4

1891	6	10	10	13.63	3	4	2
1892	5	19	3	15.53	2	19	9
1893	5	13	7	12.44	3	2	7
1894	5	11	5	12.73	2	19	6
1895	5	15	8	11.37	3	3	6
1896	6	1	8	12.11	3	7	5
1897	5	17	7	14.17	-	-	-

As often happens in war, Napoleon, when striking at his enemy, wounded his friend. For centuries Spain drew most of her resources from her colonies; and, as these dwindled in number, the pressure increased on those which remained. When the insurrection occurred in 1868, Cuba produced nearly one-half of the cane of the world; but for several years previously prices had ranged so low that production on the old basis ceased to be profitable. Accordingly, the concentration of property had already begun, and "numerous American and English fortune hunters, who had purchased large estates from impoverished Cubans . . . had started sugar and tobacco growing on an improved system in various parts of the island." [6]

The planters thus evicted gradually came to form a class of broken men ripe for brigandage; and though, at the outbreak of the insurrection, certain of the leaders were persons of property and position who revolted against the maladministration of Spain, the dis-

[6] *Cuba Past and Present*, Davey, p. 80.

content was always fomented by what amounted to a slow confiscation of the land.

The truth of these inferences may be demonstrated by the character of the war, which was always rural. The rebel armies, if such these marauders can be called, were composed partly of adventurers, who acted as officers, and partly of Negroes whose employment had gone with the devastation of the sugar estates. The towns never participated in the movement; and the vagrant bands who infested the hills and ravaged the plantations consisted "of a horde of civilized and uncivilized adventurers, recruited from all parts of the island, and indeed from the four quarters of the globe . . . the riffraff turned out of the neighboring islands, Americans, Mexicans, Germans, Italians, and even a few Englishmen." [7]

This convulsion lasted through nearly a generation; flickering out when business mended, and flaring up when it failed, until the final catastrophe came with the panic of 1893. Between 1893 and 1895 sugar sank about 30 per cent, and the death-agony began. The American public knows the rest.

But if the Spanish civilization in the West Indies has fallen amid blood and fire, the English shows every sign of decrepitude. Great Britain is a strong power,

[7] Ibid., p. 102.

and her police force is irresistible; but the decay of her islands is admitted. Had England retained the energy of 1805, when her conferences with her enemies were conducted at spots like Trafalgar, she might not perhaps have bartered her heritage for a sugarplum; but her people in 1870 saw life with different eyes from those of the men who fought the Napoleonic wars. Instead of being stimulated to ferocity by the Continental attack, the English took the bribe, and withdrew from the contest. Instead of accelerating their movement, they relaxed it.

The tendency of modern trade is toward consolidation because the administration of the largest mass is the cheapest. This is pre-eminently true of sugar manufacture; for, above all forms of agriculture, sugar lends itself to centralization. The chief expense of the plantation is the mill to crush the cane; and the more cane that can be crushed by a single machine, the more economical is the process. Accordingly, the only limit to the size of the modern factory is the distance it pays to carry a bulky raw material; and this depends on the perfection of the transportation. Therefore, an energetic population, pressed by competition, would normally have concentrated property on a vast scale; and the Government would have addressed itself to providing universal cheap transportation—presumably a

State system, like that of Germany or Russia. The islands are well adapted to electric tramways running down the valleys to the ports, which could draw their electricity from central powerhouses built on watercourses. At the ports the produce can be collected by coasters; and such is substantially the method of the Boston Fruit Company in Jamaica, which has been crowned with brilliant success. These phenomena are conspicuously lacking among the British. The only railroad of Jamaica has been built at vast expense over the mountains where no traffic goes; and it charges prohibitive rates because, being bankrupt, it lacks rolling stock to do its business. Thus, the farmers are forced to haul their crops along the roads, and are expected to compete with German bounty-fed beet, carried at a fixed minimum tariff on State lines. The British Government has even gone farther, and has discouraged quick transportation to America. Plant made a proposition to extend his service from Florida to Jamaica; but the offer was declined. Lastly, Great Britain, while abandoning the colonists to the Germans, has used them to support an exceedingly costly system of government, whose chief object has been to provide a long pay roll and pension list. This system has broken down. It has proved only less disastrous than that of Spain.

On the other hand, the native population has shown

little recuperative energy. Instead of being consolidated, the estates have been abandoned when they ceased to pay, although throughout the islands well-handled and well-situated sugar lands have never yet proved unprofitable, and although both Government and people are aware that nothing can ever replace the sugar industry, both on account of its magnitude and of the employment it gives to labor.

Yet, when allowance has been made for West Indian inertia, the stubborn fact remains that the influx of fresh capital and fresh blood has been arrested by the fear of progressively increasing sugar bounties and correspondingly decreasing values. Men do not venture their fortunes in speculation when they know that the power, which should protect them, has accepted a bribe to abandon them to an adversary bent on destroying the industry in which they are engaged.

The inference from these considerations is that the British Empire in the Western tropics is disintegrating, and that it is disintegrating because a governing class has arisen in the Kingdom which, from greed, has compounded with its natural and hereditary enemy. The advent of this class has wrought great changes in the past, and is full of meaning for the future. Already it has precipitated revolt in Cuba, defeat for Spain, expansion for America, and corresponding decline for England. Should the future resemble the past, and the conditions of competition remain unchanged, the Caribbean archipelago must, probably, either be absorbed by the economic system of the United States or lapse into barbarism. Now the current sets toward America; and the absorption of any considerable islands will probably lead to the assimilation of the rest; for the preference of the products of any portion of the archipelago by the United States would so depress the trade of the remainder as to render civilized life therein precarious. Should the foregoing deductions be correct, it is evident that the expansion of the United States is automatic and inevitable, and that, in expanding, she only obeys the impulsion of nature, like any other substance. If the Republic moves toward further concentration, it is because the world about it moves; and if it changes its institutions, it is because the conditions of modern competition demand it.

A century ago, when communication was costly and slow, the capital cities of the two competing economic systems might lie side by side on the Seine and on the Thames, and they might approach each other thus closely because the spheres of which they were the centers were relatively small. Since then, as movement has quickened, these spheres have enlarged until the Continental, having stretched eastward overland until it has reached Manchuria, now seeks to consolidate all northern and eastern China. Meanwhile, the maritime, leaving the North American continent in its rear, is drawing to itself the islands of the Pacific, is fortifying the approaches thereto, and is preparing to ascend the Yangtse and the Ho-hang-ho.

But, in proportion as the bulk of the masses of which they were once the core has dilated, the position of London and Paris has become eccentric. Therefore the focuses of energy of modern society tend to separate, the one drawing toward the confines of Russia, the other gravitating toward America; and, as they separate, competition adjusts itself to the new equilibrium. The burden of the struggle between the two systems is passing from the shoulders of Englishmen and Frenchmen, who have borne it in the past, to those of Americans and Germans, who must bear it in the future. Already, the heat generated by contact at the circumference of these rival masses presages possible war.

Furthermore, if America is destined to win in this battle for life, she must win because she is the fittest to survive under the conditions of the twentieth century. From the dawn of history, nature has always preferred those organisms which worked most economically at the time her choice was made. Men may be able to live most cheaply because they can conquer, confiscate, and enslave, like the Romans, or because they can toil longest on the least nutriment, like the Chinese; but, among Western races, who vary little in tenacity of life, those have proved the most economical who have attained the highest centralization combined with the greatest rapidity of movement. Hence, if Americans are to outstrip their opponents, they must do so by having a compacter and more flexible organization and shorter and cheaper communications. On their side, Russia and Germany are exerting their whole strength. They hope to economize in their administration by reducing their armaments, just as we increase ours; and they are completing a railroad to Peking, by which they propose to centralize the greatest mass of cheap labor in the world, on the spot where mineral resources are richest.

Nothing under the sun is stationary: not to advance is to recede; and to recede before your competitor is ruin. Unless the maritime system can absorb and consolidate mankind as energetically as the Continental, the relation which the two have borne to each other since Waterloo must be reversed.

The West Indies are gravitating toward the United States; therefore, the West Indies must be consolidated, and the lines of communication with them shortened and cheapened. Therefore, a canal to the Pacific must be built, and Central America must become an integral part of the economic mass, much as Egypt has become a part of England in order to guarantee her communications with India. Lastly, adequate outlets for the products of this huge center of energy must be insured; for, should production be thrown back on our hands by the closing of Asiatic markets to us, or should our industries be crippled by attacks such as those which have ruined the West Indies, we shall suffer from having been the weaker, and our civilization will wither like the civilizations which have preceded it.

If expansion and concentration are necessary, because the administration of the largest mass is the least costly, then America must expand and concentrate until the limit of the possible is attained; for Governments are simply huge corporations in competition, in which the most economical, in proportion to its energy, survives, and in which the wasteful and the slow are undersold and eliminated.

The Decay of England

HUMAN society is a complete living organism, with circulation, heart, and members. The heart lies at the seat of international commercial exchanges, the circulation flows through the arteries of trade, and the members usually show more or less vitality in proportion to their direct relations with the heart. Moreover, this organism, like all others, is never perfectly quiescent, but ceaselessly contracts or expands, and as it does so, the course of its circulation and the position of its heart shift to correspond with its varying bulk. This shifting of the geographical position of the heart is, perhaps, the most serious catastrophe with which mankind has to cope; for the movement of the economic capital of the world from any given abiding place indicates that the equilibrium of society has been disturbed, and that the entire relations of the race must be readjusted before a new equipoise can be attained.

These readjustments have always been called revolutions, and most of the worst convulsions of history have occurred during the intervals of transition when the seat of empire, having abandoned one abode, had not yet fixed upon another. The last of these spasms began in 1793 and ended with Waterloo; then came a calm, and from 1815 onward for about two generations, London assumed daily, more and more undisputedly, the functions of the economic capital, and Great Britain became more admittedly the seat of empire. This period of preponderance lasted until 1890, since which time an impression has gained ground that England is relatively losing vitality, that the focus of energy and wealth is shifting, and that, therefore, a period of instability is impending.

Should this supposition be true, no event could be more momentous to America; for, if the Western continent is gaining at the cost of the Eastern, the United States must shortly bear the burden England has borne, must assume the responsibilities and perform the tasks which have within human memory fallen to the share of England, and must be equipped accordingly. Such a proposition may well occasion anxiety, since few Americans can feel confident that the antiquated administrative machinery we have inherited from the last century is adapted to meet such a strain. In that case social reorganization may lie before us; and indeed the path to supremacy has seldom proved smooth.

Nevertheless, fears are unavailing, if reason for fear

there be. Timidity never yet averted disaster, while safety comes from an intelligent appreciation of situations as they arise, and from preparation for emergencies. Questions of domestic administration can be relegated to the future to which they appertain; for the moment our foreign relations, which will brook no delay, may well absorb our attention, for they involve peace and war. For nearly a hundred years England has acted as the containing power, or balance wheel, of the world; but if England is really losing her vitality, she can no longer be relied upon to perform that function, and until a new equilibrium can be attained each community must fight for itself in every corner of the globe. The great overshadowing question of the hour, therefore, is whether Great Britain is showing symptoms of decay.

Although down to the crash of 1890, when the Barings fell, Great Britain appeared to perform her accustomed office with ease, signs were not wanting that a change had previously set in. The onward movement of civilization is as automatic and resistless as any other process of nature, and may, perhaps, be aptly compared to the path of a cyclone, whose highest velocity is attained within the central vortex, the tendency toward calm increasing in proportion to the distance from the point of disturbance. The moment the vortex advances, the agitation at the spot from whence it departed begins to subside, until complete tranquility, or even death, supervenes. For example, the vortex of civilization reached London from the banks of the Tigris, by way of Constantinople, Venice, Antwerp, and Amsterdam. Amsterdam and Antwerp are calm, Venice and Constantinople are torpid, while Ctesiphon, on the Tigris, is a ruin in a desert. Accordingly, one method of determining whether the world's capital is in movement or at rest, is to ascertain whether the population of the country of its apparent domicile maintains its activity relatively to rivals, or whether it tends to become lethargic. The present purpose is to apply this test to Great Britain, and formulate the result obtained.

During the first portion of this century the Englishman stood forth as the personification of energy. In war, in commerce, in intellectual activity, in industry, in invention, he challenged all comers, and on the whole, surpassed all opponents. Perhaps no purely literary period in any nation in modern times has been more splendid than that which began with Burns and Scott, and ended with Newman, Macaulay, and Dickens. Of the English railroad and the English colony it is unnecessary to speak, and for many years English manufacturers met with no competition. The English Navy and Army made their record at Trafalgar and Waterloo.

Nearly a generation ago, however, and about the moment when Germany began to rise in economic importance after the overthrow of France, men began to notice that the English were losing their initiative. For example, for more than two decades contractors have complained, with growing vehemence, that English firms were dilatory, and that Englishmen would seldom leave their dinners or their sport for business.

The next phenomenon that attracted attention was that Germans and Americans, who were more diligent, succeeded where Englishmen failed; that, for instance, Americans found no difficulty in making the island of Jamaica profitable, after its owners had given it up as hopeless. Long since, the casual German and American tourist has habitually noticed the slackness of London tradesmen, and the amount of time given to amusement. Shops open late and close early, nothing is done on Saturday, and on Monday labor is apt to be demoralized, the inference being that somebody must lose in proportion to the loss of time. Nevertheless, such observations were not taken very seriously, and are now only noteworthy in the light of recent experience. The first real shock to confidence came with the failure of British agriculture, and with the long series of consequences which followed therefrom.

After the war of 1870, Germany demonetized silver, and a contraction of the currency followed which depressed prices universally, but especially those of agricultural products. On account of an inferior railway system, which has never been modernized, of an expensive tenure of land, and an intellectual inelasticity in respect to habits, English farmers proved unable to cope with this situation; estates went out of cultivation, and the United Kingdom, for its chief supplies of food, became dependent on foreign countries. Had this been all, the result might not have been serious; for had the decline in agriculture been compensated by an advance in industries, the loss in one direction might have been balanced by gain in another; but such was not the case. At the very moment when agriculture collapsed, the productive energy of the people showed symptoms of decay. The ratio of exports to the individual has never since stood so high as in the early 'seventies, while on the other hand the tendency toward increasing extravagance has been marked.[1]

Even in the Middle Ages the English were famous for high living, and this failing has not waned with time. The average consumption of beer to the individual, for instance, grows at the rate of 1 per cent per year, yet no one can have glanced at Dickens' novels and not have noticed the inordinate part which drinking must have played in English life sixty years ago.

[1] See on this subject the statistics in *England's Decadence in the West Indies*, pp. 71, 72, 73.

In short, the British, as a nation, are wasteful and profuse. Americans are not frugal, and still the returns of the savings banks of the United Kingdom, in 1898, showed that the economies of England, Scotland, and Ireland only exceeded those of the state of New York by about $67,000,000 while the totals represented an average accumulation of $136 for Americans, as against $23.60 for British subjects. (For the purpose of comparison both populations are taken at the figures for 1890.)

The effect of this lavish outlay for indulgences has been to cause the value of English imports to gain on the value of exports, until the annual adverse balance approximates $800,000,000, and to meet this enormous deficit a liquidation of foreign investments has apparently been long in progress. Few unprejudiced observers have ever doubted that much of the financial stringency which prostrated Argentina, Australia, and America between 1890 and 1897 originated in the withdrawal of English capital, a withdrawal which, so far as America is concerned, has not been checked by the return of prosperity, but promises to continue until the fund is exhausted.

Long after foreigners had begun to ponder these matters, Englishmen treated them with contempt. Recently, notwithstanding, their self-complacency seems to have been ruffled, for Mr. Giffen has published a very long pamphlet, to demonstrate that an apparently overwhelming deficit is the surest sign of rising opulence. However this may be, statistics alone carry little weight, for they can be twisted to prove anything; the chief value of statistics lies in their aptitude to explain accepted facts. Possibly England may be growing rich; France is richer now than in 1870, and yet France is declining. In human affairs all is relative.

Turning from commerce to literature, education, transportation, or industry, the same suggestive slackness will be found to prevail. This generation has produced little of high literary excellence; even political economy, which, since the days of Adam Smith has been the chosen field of Great Britain, has proved barren. Thought in London still smacks of Cobden and a former generation, and Bagehot, perhaps, was the last suggestive writer who dealt with these subjects. Furthermore, no one acquainted with the two systems would compare English with German schools, any more than students would measure English critical scholarship by the Continental standard. The proof is that few foreigners, who are in earnest, frequent Oxford or Cambridge, while Vienna, Berlin, and Paris are thronged.

In the matter of transportation, it is notorious that the British railways stand substantially where they did twenty years ago, while the advances in America have been bewildering; and no one doubts that Carnegie could undersell every iron concern in the United Kingdom if so disposed. Strangest of all is the mental inertia which prevents the Englishman from comprehending the world about him. He still looks on American competition as an accident, he still regards his railways as the best, he is still pleased with the results attained at his universities, he is satisfied with the place he holds; he does not care to change. He fails to perceive that beyond the boundaries of Great Britain the methods of organization and administration have altered throughout the world, while within they tend to fixity.

Approached from this standpoint the Boer War merits an attention it has not received, for its bearing on the whole future relations of the world cannot be overestimated. Moreover, the time has now come when it can be treated as a thing of the past, and its events can be analyzed calmly.

At the outset it must be premised that morality lies entirely beyond the scope of this inquiry. The justice or injustice of the war conducted by the United Kingdom is immaterial. The present investigation is directed simply toward establishing, if possible, the force which propelled England in the direction of an inevitable collision, and also toward measuring the amount of energy developed by her at the point of impact. It is a problem in dynamics.

The Boers, a sluggish, primitive people, for years retreated before the advancing British until they entered the inhospitable region north of the river Vaal, which offered no inducement to colonization. Nevertheless, friction continued between the neighboring communities, and in 1877 the English annexed the whole district. Subsequently, the Boers revolted, and, in consequence of their revolt, Great Britain conceded them substantial independence, simply because the value of the Transvaal did not justify the cost of conquest. Convinced of this fact, Mr. Gladstone declined to allow himself to be goaded into war by the humiliation of Majuba Hill in 1881, and there is no ground for supposing that Mr. Gladstone's policy would not have been the policy of all subsequent cabinets, had not the discovery of gold in 1884 revolutionized the aspect of South Africa. That event proved decisive, for from the moment that great properties became developed at Johannesburg, an unceasing dispute raged over the division of profits between the capitalists, at whose head stood Cecil Rhodes, and the Boers, represented by Mr. Kruger. At length the former decided that it would be cheaper to subdue the Dutch republic than to pay the taxes and submit to the restrictions on industry imposed by, what they considered, a feeble and retrograde Government.

In this conclusion Rhodes was justified by all the evidence, at the time, obtainable, and he was also justified in attempting the task alone, since he had effective support within the British Cabinet, and permission to use British officers to command his expedition.

Indeed, nothing looked simpler than the conquest of this petty state, and today, save the impediment of distance and the cost of supplies, no serious obstacle appears to have hindered the invasion. The Boers are brave and hardy, and doubtless would make good soldiers were they well organized and led; actually they are a handful of peasants, and they have the strength and weakness of peasants. They can ride fast from point to point, and defend themselves well, if not too sharply attacked, but they are without cohesion, initiative, or invention. They cannot advance and they cannot concentrate. All this was well known in 1895, and influenced by such knowledge, Cecil Rhodes conceived his famous raid. In his scheme he certainly had the support and approval of influential members of Lord Salisbury's Government. The evidence on this point is conclusive. In the first place, so extensive a plot could hardly have escaped the knowledge of the authorities, especially as Rhodes was Prime Minister of the colony; in the second, Jameson's force was led by British officers, some high in rank, who escaped punishment for so serious a crime; lastly, Mr. Chamberlain has always acted as Rhodes's attorney. Chamberlain not only organized a parliamentary committee to smother inquiry, but he vouched for Rhodes's character, continued him in the Privy Council, and actually prevented any compensation being paid for the damages done the Boers during the invasion. Most significant of all, this last year, when accused of participation in the raid, and when the reputation of England for integrity, to say nothing of his own, hung in the balance, when he had everything to gain and nothing to lose by proving himself innocent, he resolutely insisted on silence.

His course will bear but one interpretation, and is chiefly interesting as showing the early date at which the interests he represented acquired control of the Government. From long before the Jameson raid, it appears certain that the resolution had been formed to dominate the Transvaal; peaceably if possible, forcibly if necessary.

In the light of Mr. Balfour's famous speeches at Manchester last January, it seems futile to go into the evidence to disprove the theory that the grievances of British subjects at Johannesburg caused the war. The chief of these grievances was the alleged denial of the franchise; but the franchise was conceded in vain. However, on this point it may suffice to quote from the *Economist*, which, however it may stand in regard to ability, is certainly both conservative and honest.

In the first place, Mr. Balfour practically declares that the Government misled the Boers; and in the second, place, that it misled the British people. Let us quote his own words: "If you consider," said he, "as I had to consider, the balance of competent opinion upon the South African question, while few men were rash enough to hazard the prophecy that the South African question would ultimately culminate in war, for the present, at all events, the probability was that we should obtain such rights for the Outlanders in the Transvaal as should at least tide over the present year and the present difficulty until perhaps some period arrived when . . . it might suit the Boer leaders to precipitate a struggle from which they hope . . . to reap . . . advantage." We read this sentence with amazement. Who does not recall the Bloemfontein Conference, at which it was distinctly laid down by Sir Alfred Milner, representing the British Government, that the franchise question was the sole key to the situation? . . . The public knows how the Transvaal conceded all that Sir Alfred Milner asked for, on the understanding that its own autonomy was not disputed or interfered with; and, according to Mr. Chamberlain, it was only due to a "misunderstanding" that that arrangement was not made the basis of peace. But now Mr. Balfour tells us in effect that the Government was not serious in its alleged belief that the franchise question was at the basis of the controversy. The franchise was a *ballon d'essai;* it was used as a mere instrument of controversy, the Government believing that it would tide things over for a year, and that then the inevitable war would break out. The Boers have not had much reason to appraise our diplomatic methods at a high value, but they will assuredly have even less after this extraordinary confession of Mr. Balfour.[2]

Evidently a sentimental enthusiasm, prevailing among the constituents of Lord Salisbury's colleagues in the Cabinet, to undertake a crusade on behalf of suffering Englishmen in the antipodes, was not the force which precipitated hostilities. If that force is to be discovered, it must be sought deep down in the very bowels of English society; it will then be found to have been generated by the pressure of the struggle for existence, a pressure which is the origin of all great movements among human beings.

Probably for two decades prior to 1899 Great Britain had not been upon a paying basis; her investments had been unfortunate, and her enormous adverse trade balance had eaten into her surplus accumulations. Each year the need of gold to pay creditors had grown more pressing, until at length, unconsciously to her-

[2] The *Economist,* January 13, 1900, p. 34.

self, and to Europe at large, the United Kingdom had drifted into a position similar to that of Spain in the early sixteenth century, when Spain, stimulated by precisely the same need for gold, exhausted first Mexico and Peru, and finally Flanders.

Before 1880 the English gentry invested their means very largely either in native farming land or in American or Australian securities. When the rent of land fell off in 1879, economy became imperative, but prodigality is not confined to any rank in English life: the aristocracy is as disinclined to self-denial as the proletariat; and, after an interval, realization of capital began. By 1886 the limit of endurance seems to have been reached, for the liquidation of loans then attained large proportions, as is indicated by the liberal remittance of gold to the United Kingdom, at the very moment when exports of merchandise were declining and imports were increasing. Then came the great period of insolvency between 1890 and 1894, in Argentina, Australia, and America, during which time many hundred millions of the best paying property owned by Englishmen passed out of existence. Accordingly, about the time the South African mines acquired celebrity, a large portion of the influential classes were in straits to pay their debts, as the scandals which arose relative to the use of famous names in promoting questionable companies sufficiently proved. Under such conditions Cecil Rhodes and his fellow-operators experienced little difficulty in obtaining complete control of fashionable society, both in and out of Parliament, while the City had plunged deeply in mining stocks. Therefore, Court, Parliament, and City alike burned to boom "Kaffirs," and nothing appeared to hinder an unexampled boom but a handful of Dutch peasants in the heart of Africa. London dreamed that, under English government, dividends would be doubled.

The interests represented by Rhodes and Chamberlain anticipated rapid and cheap success, nor was such an anticipation unreasonable. The whole power of what was then supposed to be a highly military and perfectly administered empire, stood pitted against thirty or forty thousand unorganized peasants, without cavalry, field artillery, or trained officers. For fourteen years, ever since the campaign for the relief of Gordon at Khartoum, successive Cabinets had pressed military reorganization, until all that British talent could do had been done, and officials had pronounced the Imperial Army, for its size, to be, perhaps, the most formidable force in existence. German officers have always expressed their incredulity, but outside the German staff few, a year ago, suspected the truth.

Viewed apart from prejudice, the performance of the British in Africa hardly compares favorably with that of France in 1870. Perhaps in want of foresight and incapacity of officers the two countries may not have been unequal; but in actual conduct in the field the French probably showed themselves the superior. Attack has usually been considered the strong point of the British, and all the evidence goes to show that during the campaign the British soldiers have not made a determined onset. Nor can there be a question about the criterion of resolute fighting. In the time of Frederick the Great, no commander felt justified in abandoning an assault until he had sacrificed from a quarter to a third of the assaulting column, and this ratio has remained the standard down to the present day. At Bunker Hill the British lost 1,050 out of a total of 3,000. At Waterloo Wellington lost 6,932 English out of a total of 23,990; at Plevna out of 75,000 infantry present, and 60,000 actually engaged, more than 18,000 were killed or wounded, and the Comte de Paris calculated that at Gettysburg 27 per cent of the Federal and 36 per cent of the Confederate Army fell, while among the Confederates were 17 generals. Positions cannot be carried without bloodshed, but from such slaughter as marked the battles of our Civil War the modern Englishman appears to recoil.[3]

[3] Certainly in view of the record of British courage and heavy losses in the two world wars, Brooks Adams' implications in this section cannot be accepted without reservation. But it is nevertheless true that modern England cannot afford a high battle-casualty rate.

War is the last and most crucial test of a nation's energy, and from the days of Cressy to those of Trafalgar, the English yielded to none in ferocity and obstinacy on the field of battle. The South African campaign has, on the contrary, throughout, been marked by inertia and feebleness.

Not to speak of the numerous surrenders of large detachments to inferior numbers under conditions which indicated panic, the pitched battles furnish material for reflection. Repulses have been so frequent that the British have accepted them as demonstrating a principle of warfare, and are now convinced that, under modern conditions, an attack in front upon the entrenchments of a resolute enemy is impracticable. And yet it may be doubted whether the British in a single case of supposed repulse have delivered a determined assault, or indeed any assault at all. The three most celebrated examples of such defeats were Gatacre's reverse at Stormberg, Methuen's at Magersfontein, and Buller's at Colenso. On each of these occasions the commanding general formed his men in solid columns and, without reconnoitering the enemy, or in any way ascertaining his exact position, marched in the direction in which the Boers were known to lie until his troops came within point-blank range. On receiving a volley or two, some men fell, though the loss has seldom been large, and then the assaulting force was withdrawn.

Buller's casualties at Colenso amounted to 1,114, of whom 348 were prisoners. To put the figures in the usual form, he lost 7 per cent of the force engaged, but less than 5 per cent in those killed and wounded. France may have betrayed weakness in 1870 but, until the destruction of her army at Sedan, never such weakness as this.

At Gravelotte, Bazaine brought 120,000 troops into action, holding 35,000 in reserve. He lost 14,795, about 10 per cent of the whole army, and above 12 per cent of those contingents actually under fire. At Vionville, the French numbered 138,000; they lost 879 officers and 16,128 men were killed and wounded, again over 12 per cent. At Sedan, out of 140,000 soldiers engaged, 17,000 were killed and wounded—still 12 per cent.

Each of these actions indicates double the energy of the British at Colenso, nor was it until the French were reduced to militia, as in the sorties from Paris, that their casualties fell to the ratios of the late war. Such was the performance of a people whom the English themselves have judged, because of their military disasters, to be far advanced toward decay; but when it comes to comparing the campaigns of Methuen, Buller, or Roberts, who failed to carry Cronje's camp though outnumbering the adversary ten to one, with the famous onslaughts of recent times, the disparity is startling.

Comment is superfluous. The causes which have shaped the course of the British campaign in Africa are apparent; and yet the military reverses which have been sustained are the least impressive aspect of this phenomenon. All armies occasionally meet defeat, none ever maintains a uniform standard of excellence, but seldom before has a great nation accepted with complacency such battles as Colenso as the measure of her soldiers' prowess.

Significantly enough, the heaviest losses suffered have been through prisoners captured in routs like Nicholson's Nek, where troops have surrendered after so slight a resistance as to indicate an inferior stamina among the men. Lord Roberts, himself, has intimated that the retreat from Spion's Kop savoured of something more questionable than an error of judgment, and Methuen's attempt to relieve Kimberley is one of the most extraordinary military operations on record.

Some 5,000 Boers appear to have held the Spytfontein Hills between Kimberley's garrison of about 4,000 and Methuen's army at the time of his repulse numbering at least 12,000, and with constant reinforcements afterward. Yet Methuen, though more than thrice as strong as his enemy, lay for two months passive, with a level approach to the town open before him; an approach as practicable, so far as is known, in December, as in February, when Roberts marched along it unopposed. Certainly Rhodes judged it to be so and stated his opinion bluntly in the famous despatch which nearly caused his arrest: "Your troops have been for more than two months within a distance of a little over twenty miles from Kimberley, and if the Spytfontein hills are too strong for them, there is an easy approach over a level flat." Roberts himself did not dare to advance against this petty detachment of Boers until he had collected 50,000 men; and there is something startling in the passionate exultation with which London received the news that 4,500 Dutch peasants had surrendered, through lack of supplies, to 45,000 imperial troops, after having victoriously defied their onset for a week in the open field.

In justification of their failure the English have maintained that modern weapons have made the attack in front impossible. Possibly this may be a correct judgment in regard to the British Army as at present organized, but it certainly was not true of the American Army at Santiago, where the assaulting column had, probably, to say the least of it, as many difficulties to overcome as Buller faced at Colenso. The Americans were practically without artillery. Our Spanish War was not remarkably ferocious. Americans would be the last to compare it with the campaigns of the Wilderness or of Vicksburg, and yet the fighting in Cuba was much more severe than in Africa. At El Caney and San Juan the Spanish lines were carried by assault with a loss of about 12 per cent of the entire army engaged; the Spanish at El Caney leaving more than one-half their men dead in the trenches. The Boers have never defended themselves like this. On the contrary, they have always retired when the fire became deadly. They have never taken the offensive. They have never struck at their adversaries' rear; they have never seriously interfered with his communications; they have never destroyed their own railroads as they fell back; they have never laid waste the country; they have never shown a disposition to die in the last ditch. In the Civil War, South Carolina lost over 23 per cent of her entire military population, killed in battle, excluding those who died by disease or were crippled. Had the British been fought with the same determination, and had they had to deal with a foe as fierce and active as Stonewall Jackson's Southerners, their position would have been precarious even had they called forth all the energy of which the empire seems today to be capable.

Viewed as a whole, the campaign in South Africa tends to confirm the German view, that English officers are incompetent because they are lazy and idle, and therefore ignorant; and that the English administration is antiquated, sluggish, and corrupt.

Nor in drawing a parallel between England in 1899 and France in 1870 must the capital consideration be omitted that, though after the Mexican expedition the condition of the French Army was admitted to be unsatisfactory, no attempt, before the German War, had been made at reorganization. Almost the opposite was the case in England. In 1899 the British Army represented the final result of fourteen years of continuous effort by the best administrative ability at the disposal of the Government. More particularly, ever since the Jameson raid in 1896, attention had been given to preparations for an invasion of the Transvaal. The result of this long period of incubation has been the development of schools of strategy where General Buller has been accepted as an authority, a frontier defended by fortresses placed in disadvantageous positions and insufficiently supplied, and a staff without maps, and incapable of formulating a plan of campaign. The inexplicable weakness of these fortresses is, perhaps, one of the most astonishing developments of modern times. Had they been moderately well placed, armed, and victualed, they might have been left to themselves, and troops might have been pushed forward toward Pretoria, through an easy country. Actually, months were lost in futile attempts to relieve places which should never have been in danger.

The Army itself presented a sorry spectacle. Without transportation adequate for rapid concentration, without competent officers or approved weapons, without proper clothing, medical supplies, or beasts of burden, without training in the most important part of the soldier's duty in the field, it would have lain at the mercy of an energetic and disciplined foe. The French committed as serious errors at Metz or at Sedan, but their losses in battle showed more tenacity in fight. Their true misfortune lay in having to face Germany.

Nevertheless, England's military reverses, however serious, are not the phenomenon which today suggests most strongly a decaying vitality, but rather that intellectual torpor which has been already mentioned, and which seems to have become characteristic of her later civilization.

In regard to their schools, their factories, their railways, and their trade, Englishmen apparently feel no serious anxiety regarding their Army; that is to say, no anxiety keen enough to stimulate a reform as drastic as that instituted by France.

In truth, the disease lies at the core of British society, and until that society is itself modified, the present standards must prevail. For example, English officers must be content to work as hard as German officers, and undergo as rigid a training; and English soldiers must be recruited from as high a class of the population as German soldiers before the English Army can hope to cope in action with such an adversary as Germany. The proposals submitted to Parliament recently by the Cabinet were trivial, but they are perhaps all that public opinion will support.

Noteworthy, however, as has been the campaign, the finance to which it has given rise is even more impressive. At the outset the Chancellor of the Exchequer assured the Commons that no cash and $50,000,000 in credit sufficed for a war involving the transport of 70,000 soldiers to Cape Town, and the subsequent march of this force through a hostile country to Pretoria. Mr. Balfour afterward defended this policy by saying that he knew Parliament well enough to understand that if the truth had been told, the representatives of the people would have preferred to keep the peace.

Supposing we had come to Parliament in the middle of August and said, "We want you to vote us immense supplementary estimates for the provision of immediate transport in South Africa; we want you to call out the reserves, we want you to embody the militia,"—what would have been the reply . . . "The proposals you make to us are inconvenient and they are costly." [4]

As the *Economist* of January 13 observed:

If there is any meaning in these words, it is that the

[4] *Times,* January 9, 1900.

Government was misleading the House and the country, as it was misleading the Transvaal.[5]

The financiering of the Boer War was based on a theory as antiquated and as tenaciously held as that of the Manchester School of Political Economy; a theory which subsequent events have exploded. Sir Michael Hicks-Beach assumed that, the United Kingdom being the chief creditor nation of the world, the Government of that nation had only to call upon its debtors, through its agent, the Bank of England, to have its coffers filled to overflowing with gold. His error lay in the fact that such conditions had vanished as completely as the supremacy of the British textiles and steel.

For nearly twenty years Great Britain has been liquidating her loans, until now little remains which can be readily turned into cash. Since the failure of agriculture in 1879, and the consequent steady drain on the United Kingdom to pay its bills for food, it has grown each year more difficult to maintain satisfactory gold balances at London. The tendency is always toward the exhaustion of the Bank reserve, and this exhaustion, creating a pressure throughout society, has generated that craving for gold which has lain at the basis of the onslaught on the Boers.

[5] The *Economist*, January 13, 1900, p. 34.

Nothing is easier than to cavil at these inferences, or, as Mr. Giffen prefers to do, ignore them. Yet certain stubborn facts always remain to be explained away. It is clear that the Bank reserve is maintained with difficulty, especially toward the New Year, and it is also clear that, instead of bullion flowing naturally toward Lombard Street as it should to a creditor during periods of settlement, bullion tends to flow away. Last year this season of strain came early and stayed late. In the first week of October the efflux from the Bank reached £1,899,778, and the reserve sank to £20,651,000. That is to say, when the invasion of Natal began, the Bank could spare no cash, and the Government had collected no hoard to fall back on. Therefore, in order not to precipitate a panic, all possible economies had to be practiced, and all payments had to be carried over Christmas. Hence, probably, that prolonged delay in shipping troops which, if the Boers had been energetic and cohesive, might have endangered Cape Colony.

Notwithstanding all palliatives the inevitable crisis came. In December, Buller's repulse on the Tugela started an incipient panic, and Lombard Street, as had always been its wont, turned toward New York for funds. In 1890, when the Barings failed, Lombard Street had drawn on Wall Street without stint, and had relieved her necessities. Last December the same measure was tried again. All the securities which Europe could gather were cast upon the market, but though prices broke, gold remained below the exporting point and recourse had to be had to loans. The correspondent of the London *Economist* thus explained the situation:

When confronted with a serious crisis in November, 1890, London turned in its embarrassment to its largest solvent debtor. American exports of merchandise had exceeded imports by only $61,000,000 in the four years preceding the Baring crash, against which was a foreign purchase of American securities and credits of perhaps $1,000,000,000 in the previous decade. Acting as a private creditor would, London, in the years following 1890, demanded settlement of America. The capital which New York had borrowed from Europe had been invested chiefly in the West, and in order to settle with Europe it was necessary for the East to recall its advances from the West. The latter found it impossible to pay promptly, and trouble followed. Nine years later London is again embarrassed ... The difficulty follows an excess of American exports in the four years preceding, of $1,500,000,000. In the same period Europe has sold back to New York a sum of American securities about equal to the amount it purchased in the decade prior to November, 1890.[6]

[6] *Economist*, January 6, 1900, p. 12.

The article then went on to state that London was bare of American securities, and that whereas "in 1891 the Bank of England could draw gold from New York" in forced settlement, now it was borrowing both our capital and our gold.

Precisely what happened in London after Colenso cannot, of course, be proved by official evidence, but common report is somewhat as follows: A run on the Bank was threatened, and application, directly or indirectly, was made without success on all sides for assistance, even to Russia. Then came an effort to contract loans.

In England, loans are usually negotiated by bill brokers, who are allowed credit at the Bank in proportion to their standing. To the extent of this credit the bill brokers can accommodate their customers, but if the credit is withdrawn they are nearly helpless. When, after Colenso, the Bank reserve fell to about £17,300,000, the Bank directors are said to have been frightened, and, beside restricting their own advances as much as possible, are reported to have notified the bill brokers that their credits would be closed. After consideration the heads of these firms are believed to have replied that if so they could no longer discount for their customers, and thus all provincial England would be paralyzed. The moment had come for determining where the world's financial capital lay. Recoil-

ing from such an extremity, the directors once more
turned to foreigners, saying in substance to the bankers
of Berlin and New York, "You cannot afford to let
us suspend, therefore you must carry us over the New
Year."

The British thus broke down even more signally in
their finance than in their campaign, but in judging
that organized capital would not permit a collapse of
credit, they were right. London had to be sustained;
but it was found on trial that America was the only
country strong enough to bear the load, and New
York the only city where gold could be had. Accordingly, though the rates of exchange indicated a loss on
the transaction, specie enough was shipped to carry the
Bank of England over the first of January, while all
settlements were postponed for sixty days. (The gold
exporting point is about 4.89. During December 1899
and January 1900, about $16,000,000 were shipped.
During December the highest rate for sixty days' exchange was $4.84½; during January, $4.85. Demand
touched $4.89 but twice during the two months. The
situation differed from the panic of 1890, when France
advanced funds. That was a surprise. Repayment was
rapid. Here resources failed, for borrowing continued.)

The same borrowing, only probably on a larger
scale, was repeated in May and June, and the second

War Loan had to be negotiated mainly in the United States in order to draw gold to London. Such facts suggest a comparison between the financial position of Great Britain in 1900 and that of France in 1871.

In the summer of 1900 Great Britain brings to an end a petty war, in a distant land, against a pitiful adversary. To pay for this war two small loans have been negotiated, together hardly exceeding $200,000,000, a sum which should be insignificant not only for the greatest financial power of the world, but for any considerable nation. Yet to pay these loans in cash, without a convulsion, proved beyond the ability of the United Kingdom, and she has had to seek aid abroad. Although the market had been sedulously prepared by the Bank, and every indulgence had been given the subscribers, the first loan of $150,000,000 turned out indigestible, and forced down the price of consols 10 per cent. In July 1899, the new 2¾ per cents sold at 107½; in July, 1900, at 97¼. More money could not be had upon the same terms, and the reason why is obvious. In England the mass of the people have little laid by; they squander their incomes as they go. In France and America, men accumulate.

In 1871 France emerged from, perhaps, the greatest European war of the century. She had been invaded, devastated, dismembered. A domestic insurrection had been suppressed amidst oceans of blood, and Paris had for months been the theater of violence and pillage. Yet such was the financial solidity of France that she easily raised the war indemnity of $1,000,000,000, besides all the other vast sums needed to discharge her debts, out of the savings of her peasants.

Herein the weakness of England lies exposed. The energy which once made the nation supreme in industry and war has declined, and has not been replaced by thrift. Even yet the expenses of the war have not been adjusted. These expenses are excessive compared to the value of the property involved. What the invasion of the Transvaal has cost nobody outside official circles knows, but a rough estimate may be formed. The Spanish War cost the United States about $10,000,000 weekly, and this is the amount reckoned on by the *Economist* as the probable outlay of England. On its face it appears inadequate, for the United States had, by comparison, little to do: few troops to send abroad, and no elaborate operations in the field. The British have transported 250,000 soldiers to the heart of Africa and have maintained them there in the dead of winter, with imperfect railway communications, and at an unparalleled sacrifice of animal life. However, let the figure stand at $10,000,000 a week. Counting active hostilities at only forty weeks, and adding to this the loss by closing the gold mines for a year, and the diamond mines for some months, together with claims for damages to the property of loyal citizens in Cape Colony, and adding also the charge for a permanent garrison and the return of the troops, a total is reached that must largely exceed $500,000,000.

Against this must be set the enhanced value of the mines. At the outbreak of hostilities the financial journals calculated that British subjects owned something less than half the stock of these properties. The output from the Transvaal has never quite reached £20,000,-000 annually. Assuming, of this £20,000,000, 25 per cent to be net profit, Great Britain's yearly dividend would be £2,500,000, or $12,500,000. Hammond, the manager, estimated the benefit of English Government at near $25,000,000 annually, but an error in his figures [7] seems to reduce this sum to $12,500,000, half going abroad. Three per cent on $500,000,000 is $15,-000,000, which is the burden incurred by the war. It is difficult to see how the nation can be eased by such a speculation, or how the recurrence of stringency in Lombard Street in December can be alleviated thereby.

If the facts here passed in review have been stated without undue distortion, but one inference can be drawn therefrom. If it be true that a relative relaxation of vigor can be traced in Great Britain, alike in private and public affairs; if a comparative subsidence of en-

[7] See *Economist* of Nov. 11, 1899, p. 1597.

ergy can be noted in the workshop and the counting-house, in the university and Parliament; if it be established that after fifteen years of labor the Army remains what it has proved itself this year; if the British attack of 1900 is to the British attack of 1800 as Buller's assault on Spion Kop was to Wellington's advance at Waterloo; if it be admitted that the Salisbury administration, though discredited at home and abroad, and smirched with sinister scandals, retains office because the nation lacks vitality to replace it, the symptoms admit of but one explanation. Nature seldom retraces her steps; Great Britain must already lie in the wake of the social cyclone.

Nor is it wonderful that England should show signs of age, for the march of civilization is constant, and the seat of empire has seldom tarried in one city more than a century before indications of displacement have appeared. Just three generations ago England conquered her supremacy at Trafalgar, and since then she has passed through the final stages of development. By 1840 the last remnants of her old free agricultural population were passing away, a population which has usually furnished the fountain of vitality to every rising race; for a hundred years, emigration has drained her of her most active blood, which has gone never to return; hence her efforts in the future can hardly be expected to equal those of the past, and society must be prepared to face the loosening of the bond which, from beyond the limit of human memory, has been the containing power of the world.

On looking back through the history of the century, no one can fail to appreciate the part played by England. It was she who determined the fate of the modern world at Trafalgar and Waterloo; it was she who checked the aggressions of Russia in Turkey and in the East; it was she who bridled the ambitions of Germany; it was she who rendered abortive the coalition forming against the United States at the outbreak of the war with Spain. In inventions, in industries, in political institutions, in scientific theories, even in social fashions, all Europe has taken her as a model. Americans, in particular, have relied on her to police the globe and keep distant markets open, allowing them to sit at home and reap the advantage without cost and without danger.

That time appears to have passed, and as England has weakened, the old equilibrium has failed. A single example will suffice of a universal movement. A year ago Great Britain attacked a few thousand obscure peasants in Central Africa. To the bewilderment of mankind her armies were defeated, her troops fled in rout, her choicest regiments surrendered. London was plunged in dismay; for the first time in her history the

Kingdom seemed to lose confidence in herself, and leaned upon her colonies. Then the world, actuated by one common instinct, closed upon the enfeebled giant. Every power had long hankered for booty, and every power exacted terms.

Germany had her price paid; France received less, but still an equivalent; but Russia took most. Openly mobilizing troops to threaten Herat, she demanded a free hand in Asia. With one stride she entered Persia, with another she set her foot on Korea, while reaching out toward the heart of China she gripped the sinking Government at Peking by the throat. The barrier had been broken down; the equilibrium of society had been deranged, and the inevitable catastrophe ensued.

The Chinese, already goaded to the uttermost by the burrowing in their entrails of the Western races in their hunt for wealth, did what the Boers had already done in Africa, and rebelled. Only, unlike the Boers, they rose with the vindictiveness and ferocity of Asiatics. Whither the revolt will lead is beyond prediction, but this much is certain: America must, in the future, fight her own battle whether she wills or no. From this inexorable decree of destiny she cannot escape. The center of the economic system of civilization is in motion, and until it once more comes to rest, tranquillity cannot return. All signs now point to the approaching supremacy of the United States, but supremacy has always entailed its sacrifices as well as its triumphs, and fortune has seldom smiled on those who, besides being energetic and industrious, have not been armed, organized, and bold.

Russia's Interest in China

ALTHOUGH Americans seem, at last, to realize that the economic centre of the world is
moving westward, and has already, probably, entered
the United States, they incline to dismiss the subject
as an abstraction; yet nothing can be more certain than
that no such migration of empire has ever yet taken
place without prolonged convulsions. Already this
generation has had a foretaste of what such a movement may portend. The old social equilibrium reached
at Waterloo passed away in 1870 when Germany consolidated after Sedan; that consolidation led to a reform of the coinage, which in its turn caused an universal derangement of values culminating in the panic
of 1893. One of the effects of that panic was a decline
in the price of sugar, which ruined the Cuban planters,
disorganized labour, and thus brought on the insurrection which ended in the Spanish War.

But the Spanish War is relatively insignificant compared with the fruits of the catastrophe of 1893 which

are now becoming visible. That catastrophe took, in the main, the form of a forced liquidation of America's foreign indebtedness, a liquidation which could not be conducted on the basis of the exportation of farm products at the prices then ruling. This necessity of providing something wherewith to meet the demands of creditors ended by stimulating cheap manufacturing, mining, and transportation, until we commanded the European market. In the end we succeeded in creating an enormous balance of trade in our favour, but in so doing we shook the civilization of the Eastern continent to its centre. As a result of our high fortune Europe is steadily sinking into economic inferiority, an inferiority especially marked in minerals, which are the core of modern industry. For the first time in human experience a single nation this year leads in the production of the precious metals, copper, iron, and coal; and this year also, for the first time, the world has done its banking to the west and not to the east of the Atlantic.

Necessarily, as America gains in momentum Europe relatively loses. The mines of the precious metals failed her long ago, copper followed, and now iron and coal have reached a price which threatens to hamper competition. Under such circumstances the people of Europe stand at bay, since ruin, more or less complete and immediate, menaces them if they fail to provide themselves with new resources as cheap and abundant as those of America.

Such resources do actually exist in the provinces of Shansi and Honan in Eastern and Central China, and it is, perhaps, mainly the attraction of this mass of undeveloped wealth which has excited the Western nations to wring successive concessions from the Chinese until the limit of endurance has been passed, and the long-expected revolt against foreigners has begun. That revolt is only one inevitable step in the progress of Chinese disintegration and reorganization. Cost what it may, sooner or later the mineral deposits of Shansi and Honan will be seized by Europeans, and he who can successfully develop these immense beds of iron and coal, by means of Chinese labour, may well hope to defy all rivals. Nevertheless, so rich a prize is not to be lightly won; too many great interests are involved; and on the decision of the fate of China may, perhaps, hinge the economic supremacy of the next century.

Not only from her geographical position, but from the magnitude of the stake she has at issue, Russia must play a leading part in the future of Asia, and during the past year her movement has been accelerated by the weakening of England. From Waterloo down to 1899 Great Britain acted as a sort of balance wheel to human society, she operated as the containing force of civilization. With the Boer War this period appears to have terminated, for the United Kingdom promises to be unequal to assume heavier burdens than those she now bears. Having failed to display either the military or the financial energy anticipated of her, by herself, her friends, or her enemies, England has stood aside, and as she has effaced herself Russia has dilated. The Russians have overflowed Persia, laid hands on Korea, and all signs pointed, in the early spring, to their design to occupy Peking, thus commanding Shansi and Honan. These provinces lie to the west and south of the capital, distant only some three or four hundred miles from ports, and containing the richest mines in the world.

The Germans have been equally aggressive, and there is ground to suspect that the growth of the ascendency of these powers over the Chinese administration, an ascendency unsupported by armed force, may have been the proximate cause of the outbreak which began in May. That outbreak may serve hereafter as the excuse for introducing garrisons.

Assuming that Russia, or Russia and Germany, can successfully occupy this region, and that England will not risk a war in opposition unless backed by redoubtable allies, a serious responsibility is cast on the United States. Apparently America must more or less completely assume the place once held by England, for the United States could hardly contemplate with equanimity the successful organization of a hostile industrial system on the shores of the Pacific, based on Chinese labour, nourished by European capital, and supplied by the inexhaustible resources of the valley of the Ho-hang-ho.

In the present juncture, therefore, no problem can be more pressing than to estimate the real energy and capacity of Russia; to try to measure the task she can accomplish alone, to ascertain the point at which she may have to seek aid abroad, and lastly to determine whether the United States can afford to allow that aid to be drawn exclusively from Europe.

Americans are apt to picture Russia as a country somewhat resembling their own; that is to say, as young and imperfectly developed, but with indefinite resources, and inhabited by a race adapted to the exigencies of modern industrial competition. Doubtless this view is held by many well-informed persons, and yet there is ground for doubting whether Russia, as now organized, ever has held, or ever can hold, her own against the West.

Far from being young, Russia is venerable, even judged by Asiatic standards. The Czar traces the source of his semidivine authority back to the traditions of Byzantium; his descent from the Greek emperors; and when London and Paris were clumps of hovels clustered on the banks of the Thames and Seine, Kiev was a rich and splendid city, frequented by merchants from many lands, endowed with famous schools, and adorned with churches whose mosaics rivaled those of Constantinople. In the first half of the eleventh century, Russia lay in the line of commerce, and stood, probably, more fully abreast of the movement of the age than she has in any other epoch. When the Eastern trade centered on the Bosphorus, the portion which sought the Baltic ascended the Dnieper to Kiev, then passed to the Lovat, and so by Lake Ladoga to the Gulf of Finland, building up Novgorod the Great on the way. But wealth, intellectual activity, and art, all withered under the competition of Italy, when Italy, stimulated by the Crusades, woke to life in the twelfth century.

During the twelfth century the focus of commercial activity moved toward Lombardy, the routes of travel changed, and as Russia became isolated, her vitality ebbed. By 1150 Venice had begun to supplant Constantinople; in 1169 Kiev suffered its first sack; while in 1224, only twenty years after the overthrow of the Greek Empire by the Franks, the Tartar domination in Russia began with the victory of the Kalka. That domination lasted three hundred years, and when it closed, Russia had grown Asiatic. During the interval the country had been severed from the West, the capital had moved to Moscow, egress to the Baltic had been barred by Germans, Poles, and Swedes, and only in 1554 did Ivan the Terrible succeed in opening the Volga as far as Astrakhan, and in navigating the Caspian. Until the eighteenth century no outlet existed on the Black Sea.

Nothing, however, remains stationary, and when the economic capital of Europe, pursuing its migrations, reached Flanders toward 1500, an unparalleled activity set in upon the shore of the North Sea. Even before Ivan conquered Astrakhan, English adventurers had penetrated to Moscow by way of Archangel and the Dwina, Archangel being, until the acquisition of Narva in 1558, the only port in the czar's dominions open to the ocean.

From this moment date the difficulties of modern Russia, for then an archaic and sluggish community entered into the vortex of competition with races more active and highly organized than itself.

To speak plainly, Russia relapsed into barbarism; but as a barbarous state it could only survive while completely separated from more advanced enemies, for communication meant equality of armament, with all the cost implied thereby, or subjugation. Therefore, Russia armed, organized, and went into insolvency; but previously, while isolated, her finances had been sound, and her population relatively prosperous.

Even as late as the time of Czar Alexis, who died in 1676, the monarch lived in splendor, maintained a sufficient army, and amassed a treasure, with a revenue of 6,000,000 roubles. (The rouble equaled about 80 cents.)

Under Peter the Great the tide of competition flowed resistlessly. By it the Russians were drawn down to the Baltic, and from the hour that Western economic standards were imposed upon them, they recognized their position as hopeless unless they could reach some sort of industrial equality with their rivals. Hence Peter surrounded himself with Dutchmen, Germans, and English; hence Catherine II sought to people the valley of the Volga with emigrants from the Palatinate; and hence those efforts of the last ten years to convert the southern Steppes into a sort of Pennsylvania, which have astonished the world.

The task attempted has been prodigious; the sacrifices exacted from the people have reached the limit of human endurance; but there is reason to believe that hitherto the effort has failed. Probably the weight of Russia as a factor in modern competition tends at this moment rather to decline than to increase.

To appreciate the crisis which Russia is facing neither its geographical position nor its past can be ignored. Russia is expensive to develop for she is cursed with costly outlets. To the south she is shut in upon an inland sea; to the north her harbors are few, distant from the richest portions of the country, and icebound. Siberia is but a narrow strip between two deserts, a strip so narrow that transportation in bulk, such as is the basis of the American system, seems forever impossible. For these reasons, Russia remains relatively now much what it was in Peter's time—an isolated mass with a highly eccentric capital, wretchedly poor, with unsatisfactory communications, schools, and administration. Lastly, to make head against these disadvantages, Russia is peopled by an archaic race; that is to say, by people who move more slowly, and therefore more wastefully, than their Western contemporaries. A race, moreover, essentially Asiatic. The Russians have patience, tenacity of life, and, possibly, adaptability to foreign guidance; but they are ignorant, uninventive, indolent, and improvident. As a result the resources of the Empire have proved inadequate to the demands made upon them; the revenue has always shown a deficit since Peter the Great, and when the finances have been subjected to a severe strain, they have collapsed.

Not only does Russia suffer from her geographical position, but her improvidence makes her, even in prosperous times, accumulate debt faster than capital. As one of her best financial writers has remarked,

"We administer our public fortune with the same

heedlessness as our private fortune. However rapidly the resources of the state augment, the expenses augment more rapidly still. Compared with the revenues, which have quadrupled, our public debt has quintupled," [1] and this was written before the advent of de Witte, the most lavish of ministers.

The Russians never have known the solvency indicated by a sound currency and an annual surplus. The present nominal gold standard is only a repetition of former expedients, and consists in the repudiation of one-third of pre-existing forced loans. Originally, the Russian standard was the silver rouble, worth $0.748, but, after the fall in silver, the Russians, being bimetallic, measured by the so-called gold rouble, though no such coin existed. Paper from the outset fluctuated, but by degrees it was brought to a tolerably steady ratio of three to two in relation to gold, until by 1894 it only varied 1.94 per cent in the course of the year. M. de Witte's reform of 1897 consisted in adopting the paper rouble as the standard and scaling down the gold coin 33 per cent. That is to say, in 1897 Russia practically canceled one rouble out of three of its existing currency, calculating that currency at its par value. (Writing historically I am obliged to use the "gold rouble" to designate the old coin of full value.)

Up to 1768 the Government used a debased copper

[1] Skalkovsky, *Les Ministres des finances de la Russie*, p. 307.

coinage and resorted to a series of desperate expedients to raise funds, but in 1768 Catherine II believed she had found an exhaustless source of wealth in paper money, which she substituted for the pre-existing tokens. It was then that the germs of the subsequent bankruptcy of 1839 were laid. This paper, called assignats, always tended to increase and to depreciate. During the Napoleonic Wars, in spite of English subsidies and a share of the French indemnity, it reached 839,000,000 roubles and had fallen in value to less than four to one in relation to silver. By 1839 the burden had grown too heavy, and Count Cancrine issued a new "credit rouble" on the basis of one to three and one-half, which constituted a repudiation of about 72 per cent. Yet these new roubles within ten years had fallen to 10 per cent discount.

Probably a complete readjustment of all debts would have supervened had not the Russians just before this time discovered that they could borrow abroad, and Gouriew availed himself so liberally of this expedient that, when he retired in 1823, he was accused of "bringing the state to bankruptcy" through the instrumentality of the Rothschilds.

The Russians are not a commercial people, consequently their finances have never been administered by men of business and have always borne an amateurish stamp. Little serious attempt at economy has ever been made, and though the people may be starving, and the currency in confusion, the Court and the Administration have always been conducted on the most lavish scale in Europe. Nevertheless, by means of the repudiation of 1839, some semblance of order was restored. That is to say, the deficit was reduced to about 30,000,000 roubles in good years, and through foreign loans a treasure was amassed large enough to lure Czar Nicholas into attempting the Crimean War. Two campaigns sufficed to exhaust the economic endurance of the Empire. In 1855 the deficit reached 262,000,000 roubles, and at the peace the paper currency amounted to 735,000,000, while 321,000,000 roubles had been extorted as a loan from all the institutions in the country which had funds. In precisely the same way Russia broke down twenty-two years later under the walls of Constantinople, and surrendered the fruits of victory, because her paper issues had attained the enormous volume of 1,200,000,000 roubles, and her 5 per cent bonds could hardly be sold in small amounts in Berlin at 26 per cent discount.

Whether in peace or war, no minister of finance during this century has ever kept the cost of government within the limits of the revenue. The bonded debt has grown under every administration, but under none so fast as under the last. The list is curious, and even startling.

In 1810 Alexander I appointed Gouriew, who held office thirteen years; besides enormous emissions of assignats, he incurred an interest-bearing debt of 185,-688,000 roubles. Cancrine, his successor, struggled with hopeless deficits, resorted to the most desperate expedients to raise funds, even selling exemptions from military service, emitted much paper, added 115,000,-000 roubles to the debt, and finally, in 1839, wiped out three-quarters of the assignats by issuing a new credit rouble at a ratio of one to three and one-half. Yet, in spite of so sharp a contraction, the new rouble fell to 3 per cent discount in 1843, and to 10 per cent in 1848. Cancrine died in 1845, and each of his three successors borrowed, more or less freely, to fill deficits, until Reutern became Minister of Finance in 1862. In his first six years his loans reached 451,000,000 roubles, and in 1864-6 he emitted 63,000,000 treasury notes. Reutern retired in 1878, and Grieg, who followed, had to set the finances in order after the Turkish War; he, Abaza, and Bunge borrowed money abroad when they could and, when they could not, issued paper at home. Thus, about the time when Vychnégradsky, de Witte's predecessor, took office, in 1887, affairs reached a crisis. The deficit continuing, severer taxation was resorted to, a panic broke out in 1888, the rouble depreciated 50 per cent, and had it not been for an exceptionally abundant harvest, a complete collapse might have occurred. A change, however, was at hand. The moment had arrived when Russia became mistress of fabulous wealth.

Previous to 1888 Russia had been mainly dependent on Germany for her capital, and this dependence had mounted to a species of subjection, for the German bankers had not scrupled to use their power as creditors to the utmost to impose a policy on the Russian Government. In 1888 the full magnitude of the change of social equilibrium wrought in 1870 manifested itself. As Central Europe had consolidated, France had been isolated, and her isolation placed her in mortal peril. This peril stimulated her people to strengthen Russia at any cost, since without an ally the Republic feared dismemberment. Thus, for several years the savings of France stood at the disposal of Russia, and the results which followed are, perhaps, without a precedent. In time of peace, between 1888 and 1897, Vychnégradsky and de Witte borrowed nearly 1,-079,000,000 roubles, of which vast sum perhaps one-half represented investments in railways, or a possibly productive outlay. In the first four years of de Witte's administration the annual disbursements rose from 900,000,000 roubles to 1,413,000,000, and for the year 1900 the budget shows a deficit of 160,600,000 roubles or $80,300,000.

It is true that the recent budgets have been made to

indicate a surplus, but this surplus is delusive. De Cyon years ago demonstrated that the apparent surpluses exhibited by M. de Witte are in reality caused by the application of the unexpended balance of old borrowings to the payment of current expenses. For example, the budget for the year 1900 shows an application of 160,000,000 roubles drawn "from the free balance of the treasury." Now this "free balance" is, in the language of de Cyon, only "the avails of unemployed loans." [2] That an actual deficit exists is proved by the advance of the debt.

Nor is the State debt the only, or even, perhaps, the heaviest burden which the Russians have assumed in their struggle for industrial development. Not being by nature inventive or mechanical, the community has striven for two centuries to domesticate foreign industries by importing foreign labor and foreign capital. To provide the necessary inducement the Russians have enacted a nearly prohibitive tariff, and attracted by the large gains which may be realized under this tariff, Germans, Belgians, and French have established plants whose profits are remitted abroad. Thus, not only is the price of all the necessities of life raised for the peasant, but the cost of internal improvement is increased. For example, the government, instead of buying its railway material in the cheapest market,

[2] E. de Cyon, *Où la dictature de M. Witte conduit la Russie,* XVIII.

buys it at home at 50 per cent advance; to pay this price to the foreigners who control the iron works, money is borrowed abroad, which money returns whence it came, and then a new loan must be negotiated in Paris or Berlin to pay the interest on the funds thus drained away.

In 1891 a French syndicate made an offer to the Russian Government to build the Siberian railway within six years, at an average cost of 40,000 roubles the verst [3] (the verst is seven-tenths of a mile), offering a guarantee that the cost should not exceed the sum indicated. The Government declined the offer and undertook the task itself, and this is a sample of what happened: The division from Cheliabinsk offered no particular difficulty, and the syndicate estimated it at 20,000 roubles the verst. It has already cost 53,000 roubles the verst, and the rails which have been laid are generally so light that they will have to be replaced before the road will carry heavy traffic.

Some of this vast excess of outlay may be attributed to the price paid for domestic material, but not all. The chief leakage is due to a weakness in Russian civilization, which vitiates all financial and administrative methods. Russian society is archaic; the system of agriculture may serve as an illustration. The basis of Russian agriculture is still communal ownership, which

[3] Ibid., 62.3.

represents an intellectual condition perhaps equivalent to that of Europe three centuries ago. Moreover, the Russians are Asiatic, and therefore less vigorous, energetic, and inventive than Western races. Accordingly, Russian peasants are miserably poor.

Estimating by aid of the figures of M. de Witte's reports, the average annual production per person approximates twenty-nine roubles; of these twenty-nine roubles upwards of twelve are absorbed in taxes, leaving about seventeen roubles as the income of the individual. Such estimates are vague, but they serve to give an idea of the impossibility of a population nearly starving, unable to buy machinery, crippled by infamous roads and insufficient railway transportation, and enervated by the rotating proprietorship of land incident to communal ownership, competing with the capitalistic methods of the Dakotas. Obviously, the value of the Russian agricultural exports must tend to decline.

For precisely similar reasons the Russian railway must be a costly and an inferior railway, because it is the product of a primitive society which generates a defective civil service. The archaic idea is to pay the official by fees; for it required an advanced economic intelligence to comprehend that it is cheaper for each citizen to be taxed for fixed salaries, than for the individual to pay for the service he needs as he might pay a doctor or a lawyer. Verres, for example, administered Sicily for what he could make out of it, and Berres and his like engendered the Empire, under which the salary system prevailed. Colbert undertook to uproot the fee system in France, and failed. The Revolution accomplished his work.

Russian officials are expected to supplement insufficient salaries by fees; hence fees, though not necessarily implying dishonesty, are universal, and entail waste and delay. The most important work, even of a routine character, may be hindered for months because some obscure official has been overlooked, who has quietly waited until the sufferer should find and pay him. Hence railways are costly, ill-organized, ill-equipped, and slackly run, and though freight rates may be nominally low, they become high through maladministration. From the palace of the czar to the hut of the peasant, the same waste, the same inertness, and the same incapacity prevail. The result is that the harder Russia is pressed by Western competition, and the more capital she is driven to borrow to invest in industrial expansion, the heavier is the burden of the nation in proportion to its resources, and the more hopeless its financial outlook.

Although between 1888 and 1897 the State debt increased about 1,079,000,000 roubles, or over 20 per cent, the interest charges only advanced 3,500,000

roubles on account of M. de Witte's success in refund-
ing at reduced rates. Nevertheless, the pressure of this
portion of the expenditure is undoubtedly severer now
than formerly, since, in the present, a far larger proportion of the debt is owed abroad, than in the
previous decade. Therefore, if in 1887 the annual payment on the debt and sinking fund came to 278,591,-
000, of which the part to be remitted abroad might
have been covered by a trade balance of 260,000,000
with perhaps a margin, a fall in the relation of exports
to imports as the process of conversion went on would
leave the country in a precarious condition.

Between 1886 and 1890 the exports of Russian merchandise exceeded the imports, on the average, by
260,100,000 roubles. Between 1891 and 1895 this balance fell to 167,554,000 roubles, and in the three years,
1896–8, to 147,812,000 roubles, and this in spite of the
high price of grain in 1897. Therefore, since the
French inflow of capital began, the balance from sales
of merchandise has decreased 43 per cent, certainly
leaving the country with a deficit on its fixed charges.
Nor is this the worst. The enormous foreign investments in industries have to obtain a profit from sales
at high prices to the peasantry or the Government, and
the money thus taken from the country is sent abroad
as regularly as State interest. Therefore, when M. de
Witte fails, as he has failed this year, to negotiate new

loans, the specie accumulated in St. Petersburg, which is the result of old borrowing, has to be exported to Paris in default of exchange. It was a recognition of this fact which probably led the Czar to call the Peace Conference, in the hope of limiting armaments and therefore expenditure.

The inference is that Russia, as now organized, is not upon a paying basis, and that Russians are ill-adapted to the exigencies of modern competition. This inference is also strengthened by the fact that the commercial interests of the Empire, in the chief cities of European Russia, are passing under the control of Germans and Jews, and that German is the language of finance.

Conversely, it seems to be generally conceded that the condition of the peasantry is deplorable. As the price of grain has fallen, taxes have risen until the margin of profit upon the average crop has dwindled to a bare subsistence, and a bad season means famine. Famine, not because bread is dear, but because the population lacks money wherewith to purchase. Hence starvation has become chronic in the Empire, and there is seldom a time when people are not dying either from hunger, or from the effects of hunger. Last winter, Bessarabia was immolated, a province which had never before known scarcity, and the bitterness of the situation lies in this, that when all has been sold and the cattle have been killed, and nothing is left to seize, the taxes accumulate, and these arrears sweep away any surplus which might remain after the next era of plenty. For this reason the inhabitants of the valley of the Volga are abandoning their farms and wandering toward the wastes of Siberia, where too often an equally miserable fate awaits them.

Such phenomena point to the conclusion that Russia must either undergo a social reorganization which will put her upon a cheaper administrative basis, or she must obtain fresh property which she can mortgage; that is to say, she must expand.

What a social revolution in Russia would portend transcends human foresight, but probably its effects would be felt throughout the world. The conservative instincts of the race are, however, very strong, and in all likelihood they will prevail until the last extremity. Assuming, therefore, that the existing status of society will remain unchanged, an alternative appears to be presented to the people.

Foreign borrowing has, apparently, been carried to something like its limit, unless new securities can be pledged, but such securities are usually the fruit of war. The most brilliant would be the Shansi minerals. The development of those deposits offers the best and, perhaps, the only chance for that industrial development for which the Russians have striven for two centuries, and hitherto failed. War is costly, but the Russians have a large treasure in gold which they can spend in expansion. If they succeed, they will have won the richest prize of modern times. If they fail, they will only arrive a few years earlier at the issue of more paper money, a measure which appears inevitable if they follow their present policy to its end; for, with the balance of trade going against them, and the interest account growing, if the reserve of specie is not used in war, it seems destined to be exhausted in paying the charges on the debt.

Should the military and agrarian party get the upper hand, as some think it has the upper hand already, an attempt would probably be made to absorb the northern provinces of China. The question is how this would affect the United States. Evidently the United States has nothing to gain by the opening up of Asia. The United States is now mistress of the situation; the United States is fast attaining a commercial supremacy heretofore unrivaled. An industrial movement in the valleys of the Ho-hang-ho and Yangtse could only tend to her embarrassment. The best thing that could happen for her would be for China to remain quiescent. But the very success and energy of America makes it unlikely that China can stay stationary; an effort at development is inevitable, and it behooves

Americans to consider whether they can safely allow that development to be wholly controlled by others. If Russia should absorb Shansi, she cannot organize it alone. She has neither the genius nor the capital. She must mortgage her property in the future as in the past, and there is a likelihood that the mortgagee will ultimately come into possession.

Even in the event of the unlikely contingency of a conflict between Japan and Russia, in which Japan should prevail, the situation would remain substantially unaltered. The Japanese, both from a financial and an administrative point of view, are fully as incapable as Russia of handling such a task unaided, and should they overcome their adversary, they would have to employ his methods in order to utilize their victory.

There remain the English, the Germans, and ourselves. The English should, probably, be dismissed from consideration; their energies are already overtaxed, and of late, save in South Africa, British capital has shown a tendency to contract, rather than to expand, its sphere of activity. The Germans, on the contrary, are aggressive, and are likely to take the present opportunity to occupy Peking in force. Were the Russians and the Germans to coalesce in order to dominate northern China, and were the country afterward to be administered by Germans, with German funds, to the exclusion of the United States, a strain of a very serious nature might be put upon America.

Our geographical position, our wealth, and our energy pre-eminently fit us to enter upon the development of eastern Asia, and to reduce it to a part of our economic system. And, moreover, the laws of nature are immutable. Money will flow where it earns most return, and investments once made are always protected. Evidently Americans cannot be excluded from China without a struggle, and they may not, perhaps, be welcomed by those who have hitherto shown most anxiety to obtain a foothold there. The Chinese question must, therefore, be accepted as the great problem of the future, as a problem from which there can be no escape; and as these great struggles for supremacy sometimes involve an appeal to force, safety lies in being armed and organized against all emergencies.

Set in Linotype Janson
Format by A. W. Rushmore
Composed by H. Wolff Book Mfg. Co.
Published by Harper & Brothers
New York and London